my revision notes

AQA AS and A-level History

THE MAKING OF MODERN BRITAIN

1951–2007

Peter Clements

Series editor:
David Ferriby

HODDER
EDUCATION
AN HACHETTE UK COMPA

Acknowledgements

The Publishers would like to thank the following for permission to reproduce copyright material.

p.17 House of Commons debate on the Suez invasion, 30 October 1956 to be reproduced in AQA AS And A Level The Making of Modern Britain 1951–2007. © Telegraph Media Group Limited 1956; **p.39** 'Beatles on the Beat', The Times newspaper 11 November 1963. Used with permission from The Times UK; **p.65** 'Police teams to fight intimidation of working miners', The Times newspaper 18 May 1984. Used with permission from The Times UK.

Every effort has been made to trace all copyright holders, but if any have been inadvertently overlooked, the Publishers will be pleased to make the necessary arrangements at the first opportunity.

Although every effort has been made to ensure that website addresses are correct at time of going to press, Hodder Education cannot be held responsible for the content of any website mentioned in this book. It is sometimes possible to find a relocated web page by typing in the address of the home page for a website in the URL window of your browser.

Hachette UK's policy is to use papers that are natural, renewable and recyclable products and made from wood grown in sustainable forests. The logging and manufacturing processes are expected to conform to the environmental regulations of the country of origin.

Orders: please contact Bookpoint Ltd, 130 Milton Park, Abingdon, Oxon OX14 4SE.
Telephone: +44 (0)1235 827720. Fax: +44 (0)1235 400454. Email education@bookpoint.co.uk
Lines are open from 9 a.m. to 5 p.m., Monday to Saturday, with a 24-hour message answering service. You can also order through our website: www.hoddereducation.co.uk

ISBN: 978 1 4718 7628 8

© Peter Clements 2016

First published in 2016 by

Hodder Education,
An Hachette UK Company
Carmelite House
50 Victoria Embankment
London EC4Y 0DZ

www.hoddereducation.co.uk

Impression number   10 9 8 7 6 5 4 3

Year   2020   2019

Cover photo © Senai aksoy-Fotolia
Illustrations by Integra
Typeset by Integra Software Services Pvt. Ltd., Pondicherry, India
Printed in India

A catalogue record for this title is available from the British Library.

My revision planner

Part 2 Modern Britain 1979–2007 (A-level only)

Introduction

Component 2: Depth Study

Component 2 involves the study of a significant period of historical change and development (around 20–25 years at AS and 40–50 years at A-level) and an evaluation of primary sources.

The Making of Modern Britain 1951–2007

The specification lists the content of this component in two parts, each part being divided into three sections:

Part 1 – Building a New Britain 1951–79
1 The Affluent Society 1951–1964
2 The Sixties 1964–1970
3 The end of the post-war consensus 1970–79

Part 2 – Modern Britain 1979–2007 (A-level only)
4 The impact of Thatcherism 1979–87
5 Towards a new consensus 1987–97
6 The era of New Labour 1997–2007

Although each period of study is set out in chronological sections in the specification, an exam question may arise from one or more of these sections.

The AS examination

The AS examination that you may be taking includes all the content in Part 1.

You are required to answer the following.
- Section A: one question on two primary sources: which is the more valuable? You need to identify the arguments in each source as well as evaluating the provenance and tone. Using your knowledge in relation to these strands, you need to assess how valuable each source is, and then reach a judgement on which is the more valuable. The question is worth 25 marks.
- Section B: one essay question out of two. The questions will be set on a topic reflecting the fact that this is a depth paper, and will require you to analyse whether you agree or disagree with a statement. Almost certainly, you will be doing both and reaching a balanced conclusion. The question is worth 25 marks.

The exam lasts one and a half hours, and you should spend about equal time on each section.

At AS, Component 2 will be worth a total of 50 marks and 50 per cent of the AS examination.

The A-level examination

The A-level examination at the end of the course includes all the content of Part 1 **and** Part 2.

You are required to answer the following:
- Section A: one question on three primary sources: how valuable is each source? You are *not* required to reach a conclusion about which might be the most valuable. You need to identify the arguments in each source as well as evaluating the provenance and tone. Using your knowledge in relation to these strands, you need to assess how valuable each source is. This question is worth 30 marks.
- Section B: two essay questions out of three. The questions will be set on a topic reflecting the fact that this is a depth paper. The question styles will vary but they will all require you to analyse factors and reach a conclusion. The focus may be on causation, or consequence, or continuity and change.

The exam lasts two and a half hours. You should spend about one hour on Section A and about 45 minutes on each of the two essays.

At A-level, Component 2 will be worth a total of 80 marks and 40 per cent of the A-level examination.

In both the AS and A-level examinations you are being tested on your ability to:
- use relevant historical information (Sections A and B)
- evaluate different historical interpretations (Section A)
- skilfully analyse factors and reach a judgement (Section B).

How to use this book

This book has been designed to help you develop the knowledge and skills necessary to succeed in the examination.
- The book is divided into six sections – one for each section of the A-level specification.
- Each section is made up of a series of topics organised into double page spreads.
- On the left-hand page you will find a summary of the key content you will need to learn. Words in bold in the key content are defined in the glossary (see pages 105–107).
- On the right-hand page you will find exam-focused activities.

Together these two strands of the book will provide you with the knowledge and skills essential for examination success.

▼ **Key historical content**

▼ **Exam-focused activities**

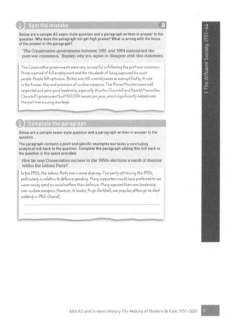

Examination activities

There are three levels of exam-focused activities as follows.
- Band 1 activities are designed to develop the foundation skills needed to pass the exam. These have a green heading and this symbol:
- Band 2 activities are designed to build on the skills developed in Band 1 activities and to help you to achieve a C grade. These have an orange heading and this symbol:
- Band 3 activities are designed to enable you to access the highest grades. These have a purple heading and this symbol:

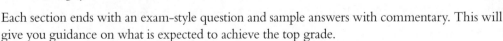

Some of the activities have answers or suggested answers on pages 109–111. These have the following symbol to indicate this:

Each section ends with an exam-style question and sample answers with commentary. This will give you guidance on what is expected to achieve the top grade.

You can also keep track of your revision by ticking off each topic heading in the book, or by ticking the checklist on the contents page. Tick each box when you have:
- revised and understood a topic
- completed the activities.

Mark schemes

For some of the activities in the book it will be useful to refer to the mark schemes for this paper. Below are abbreviated forms.

Section A Primary sources

Level	AS-level exam	A-level exam
1	Describing source content or stock phrases about value of source; limited understanding of context. (1–5)	Some comments on value of at least one source but limited response; limited understanding of context. (1–6)
2	Some relevant comments on value of one source, or some general comments on both. Some understanding of context. (6–10)	Some relevant comments on value of one or two sources, or focus only on content or provenance, or consideration of all three sources in a more general way. Some understanding of context. (7–12)
3	Some relevant comments on value of sources, and some explicit reference to focus of question, with some understanding of context. Judgements thinly supported. (11–15)	Some understanding of all three sources in relation to content and provenance with some awareness of historical context. An attempt to consider value, but probably some imbalance across the three sources. (13–18)
4	Range of relevant well-supported comments on value of sources for issue identified in question. Not all comments will be well-substantiated, and will have limited judgements. (16–20)	Good understanding of three sources in relation to content and provenance with awareness of historical context to provide a balanced argument on their value in relation to focus of question. One or more judgements may be limited in substantiation. (19–24)
5	Very good understanding of value of sources in relation to focus of question and contextual knowledge. Thorough evaluation, well-supported conclusion. (21–25)	Very good understanding of all three sources in relation to content and provenance and combines this with strong awareness of historical context to present balanced argument on their value in relation to focus of question. (25–30)

Section B Essays

Level	AS-level exam	A-level exam
1	Extremely limited or irrelevant information. Unsupported, vague or generalising comments. (1–5)	Extremely limited or irrelevant information. Unsupported, vague or generalising comments. (1–5)
2	Descriptive or partial, failing to grasp full demands of question. Limited in scope. (6–10)	Descriptive or partial, failing to grasp full demands of question. Limited in scope. (6–10)
3	Some understanding and answer is adequately organised. Information showing understanding of some key features. (11–15)	Understanding of question and a range of largely accurate information showing awareness of key issues and features, but lacking in precise detail. Some balance established. (11–15)
4	Understanding shown with range of largely accurate information showing awareness of some of the key issues and features leading to a limited judgement. (16–20)	Good understanding of question. Well organised and effectively communicated with range of clear and specific supporting information showing good understanding of key features and issues, with some conceptual awareness. (16–20)
5	Good understanding. Well organised and effectively communicated. Range of clear information showing good understanding and some conceptual awareness. Analytical in style, leading to a substantiated judgement. (21–25)	Very good understanding of full demands of question. Well organised and effectively delivered, with well-selected, precise supporting information. Fully analytical with balanced argument and well-substantiated judgement. (21–25)

1 The Affluent Society 1951–64

Conservative governments and the reasons for political dominance

The Conservative Party won the 1951 election and remained in power until 1964.

Political leaders

The principal Conservative leaders were:

- Winston Churchill (Prime Minister 1951–55). Britain's famed wartime leader, he was 77 years old by 1951, and often ill. He was mainly a figurehead leader by this time.
- Anthony Eden (Prime Minister 1955–57). He had been a long-serving Foreign Secretary. His premiership was cut short by the Suez Crisis (see page 18).
- Harold Macmillan (Prime Minister 1957–63). Macmillan presided over a massive increase in prosperity in Britain.
- Sir Alec Douglas-Home (Prime Minister 1963–64). Before he began to make his mark his government was defeated in the October 1964 election.

Domestic policies 1951–64

The Conservatives governed Britain between 1951 and 1964, but there was broad agreement between the three major parties. This was known as the **post-war consensus**.

The post-war consensus

- The importance of extensive welfare systems and the National Health Service **'from the cradle to the grave'**.
- Intervention in the economy to ensure maximum growth, fair practices and full employment.
- Foreign policy based on support for the USA and opposition to the USSR and Communism.
- Independence for the colonies of the Empire.

Conservative political dominance 1951–64

At the end of the 1951–64 **Conservative governments**, the Labour Party labelled the period as '13 wasted years'. Yet the Conservatives had retained popularity **for thirteen years** and Britain seemed more prosperous than ever before.

Reasons for Conservative success:

- Economic policies seemed successful, with minimal unemployment and significant increases in the standard of living.
- The Conservatives were associated with a new Elizabethan Age of optimism and prosperity headed by the young Queen Elizabeth II who had been crowned in 1953.
- Britain still seemed a world power, with nuclear weapons and a commendable record in the **Korean War**.
- The Conservatives maintained welfare spending, economic planning and policies to engender full employment.
- Churchill's government built 300,000 houses per year – although these were mainly for purchase rather than **public sector housing**.
- Over 6,000 new schools were built and plans were made for a doubling of university places.
- The first motorways were built with part of the M1 being opened in 1959.
- Britain became an atomic power with the explosion of the first British atomic bomb in 1952.

The Conservatives won three elections, in 1951, 1955 and 1959.

Year	Conservative Party	Labour Party	Liberal Party	Others
1951	321	295	6	3
1955	344	277	6	3
1959	365	258	6	1

The Labour Party moreover was in some disarray.

- The Party split during the 1950s, particularly in relation to defence spending. Many wanted more money spent on social welfare than defence. They opposed the development of nuclear weapons, which the leadership supported.
- Labour faced problems beyond its control, for example its popular leader Hugh Gaitskell died suddenly in 1963.
- The electorate was satisfied with Conservative rule, due to continuing prosperity, and many did not trust Labour to maintain it.

Spot the mistake a

Below are a sample AS exam-style question and a paragraph written in answer to the question. Why does the paragraph not get high praise? What is wrong with the focus of the answer in the paragraph?

'The Conservative governments between 1951 and 1964 maintained the post-war consensus.' Explain why you agree or disagree with this statement.

> The Conservative governments were very successful in following the post-war consensus. It was a period of full employment and the standards of living improved for most people. People felt optimism. Britain was still a world power as exemplified by its role in the Korean War and possession of nuclear weapons. The Prime Ministers were well respected and gave good leadership, especially Winston Churchill and Harold Macmillan. Churchill's government built 300,000 houses per year, which significantly helped ease the post-war housing shortage.

 Complete the paragraph

Below are a sample exam-style question and a paragraph written in answer to the question.

The paragraph contains a point and specific examples but lacks a concluding analytical link back to the question. Complete the paragraph adding this link back to the question in the space provided.

How far was Conservative success in the 1950s elections a result of disarray within the Labour Party?

> In the 1950s, the Labour Party was in some disarray. The party split during the 1950s, particularly in relation to defence spending. Many supporters would have preferred to see more money spent on social welfare than defence. Many opposed their own leadership over nuclear weapons. However, its leader, Hugh Gaitskell, was popular, although he died suddenly in 1963. Overall,
>
> _____
>
> _____

Reasons for the Conservatives' fall from power

Following their third victory in 1959, the Conservatives themselves were looking tired and out of touch.

- The leadership was ageing and many thought it was too unrepresentative of the **'New Britain'**. They were almost exclusively born to wealth and privilege. There were no women in government or even younger men.
- **Satirists** mocked the leading figures mercilessly. Political leaders were caricatured and often shown as ridiculous.
- Various scandals in which establishment figures had been caught spying for the Soviet Union such as the Vassall Affair rocked the government. In January 1963 Kim Philby, a trusted MI6 agent, fled to the USSR. He had been passing on sensitive information for much of his career. Although most of the misdemeanours predated Macmillan's government they inevitably reflected badly on it.
- Macmillan had sacked most of his cabinet in the so-called 'Night of the Long Knives' in 1962 to try to introduce younger figures into government – but it simply gave the impression of disunity.
- A series of sex and moral scandals, culminating in the Profumo Affair of 1963, undermined the government. John Profumo, Minister for War, admitted to lying about his affair with a much younger woman. The ensuing investigation implicated many senior establishment figures in disreputable activities and again, by implication, made the government look ridiculous.
- Macmillan himself retired in 1963, to be replaced by Sir Alec Douglas-Home who had barely time to establish himself before a general election had to be called.

Satire

The 1950s saw a general decline in deference, or respect offered to establishment figures simply because of who they were. University students had set up satirical reviews such as 'Beyond the Fringe', which lampooned leaders. These became so popular that some satirists, notably Peter Cook, moved their reviews to the West End of London where they attracted wide audiences. By the early 1960s leading exponents were appearing on TV. The programme *That Was The Week That Was*, known as TW3, first appeared in 1962 and made presenters such as David Frost household names. When it was cancelled in the election year 1964, one reason offered was that voters might be too influenced by its content.

Replacement of Macmillan

The way in which Macmillan was replaced by Sir Alec Douglas-Home suggested antiquated methods and privilege. The method of replacing a Conservative leader was to sound out senior colleagues to ascertain who they would serve under; there was no semblance of democracy. The two most able candidates in 1963 were former Chancellor R.A. Butler and Lord Hailsham, a senior peer. However, a compromise candidate was chosen in Sir Alec Douglas-Home, then known as Lord Home, who had to renounce his peerage in order to serve. Although this was the final time a Conservative leader was appointed in such a way, it served to show how out of touch the party was with current changes in society.

The 1964 election

Labour won the 1964 election by an overall majority of four. Its leader Harold Wilson spoke of technological and scientific developments in terms of **'white heat'**. While the narrow victory suggested to some a falling off of support for the Conservatives rather than enthusiasm for Labour, many Labour candidates seemed more in tune with the times than the Conservatives.

General election results 1964

Party	Number of Seats
Labour	317
Conservative	304
Liberal	9

Support or challenge

Below is a sample AS essay-style question that asks how far you agree with a specific statement.

Divide the statements into the following.

1 Those that support the statement in the question.

2 Those that disagree with the statement in the question.

'By the early 1960s the Conservative government of Harold Macmillan was increasingly out of touch with developments in Britain.' Explain whether you agree or disagree with this view.

	Support	Challenge
The Conservative governments were very successful in winning elections during the 1950s, including that of 1959.		
The Conservatives had been in power since 1951 and were increasingly looking tired by the early 1960s.		
There were no women in government.		
People voted Conservative because Britain was prosperous and they did not trust Labour to maintain the economic successes.		
The Conservatives' electoral victory of 1959 saw their overall majority increased from 58 seats in 1955 to 100 in 1959; this hardly suggests a government that was out of touch.		
Many members of the government were elderly and were not in tune with the changes that had been taking place in British society.		
Macmillan dismissed many of his cabinet in 'The Night of the Long Knives' in 1962 with the aim of making his government younger and more in touch. However, this simply served to emphasise the divisions within it.		

Spot the mistake a

Below is part of the answer to the question in 'Support or challenge' above. Why does this paragraph not achieve Level 4? Once you have identified the mistake, rewrite the paragraph so it displays the qualities of Level 4. The mark scheme on page 7 will help you.

The Conservatives governed Britain between 1951 and 1964 and won three elections in 1951, 1955 and 1959 so they couldn't have been that much out of touch. If they had been people wouldn't have voted for them. Nevertheless, people also voted for them because of the post-war consensus, a broad agreement between the three major parties about policies such as the maintenance of the welfare state and economic growth. People voted for them because they supported these policies. They did not vote Labour because Labour was split over, for example, defence spending. Besides this, Britain was prosperous and the Conservatives took credit for a successful economy. People didn't feel Labour could be trusted to maintain this prosperity. The Conservatives were lampooned, however, in satirical magazines and they did look rather old and fuddy-duddy. The scandals did not help — the Minister for War was having an affair with a much younger woman. These factors helped to discredit the government but that doesn't mean they were out of touch.

Economic developments

The post-war boom

The period of Conservative government from 1951 to 1964 saw a period of economic growth and unprecedented rises in living standards. However, it also saw underlying problems that would resurface significantly in the ensuing decades.

Butskellism

There was little difference between Labour and Conservative views on the economy – policies were known as **'Butskellism'**, an amalgam of the names of the Conservative Chancellor of the Exchequer R.A. Butler (1951–55) and Labour Shadow Chancellor and future party leader Hugh Gaitskell. The aims were as follows.

- Maintenance of full employment and economic growth.
- Continued development of the welfare state.
- Maintenance of defence commitments and nuclear weaponry.

The British economy grew as did others in western Europe as a result of **Marshall Aid** and the growth of exports. However, there were always problems with the following.

- Balance of payments issues: Britain imported more than it sold abroad so its balance of payments was always in deficit (by 1961 to the tune of £95 million).
- Britain could not afford to build a modern, competitive economy, develop the welfare state and maintain its defence commitments.
- Growing inflation: people spoke of **'stagflation'** – or continued price rises despite a downturn in the economy.
- Industrial relations: as inflation grew, workers demanded pay rises in excess of price rises.

As a result of this Britain's debts increased year on year – by 1957 they were £540 million and in 1964, £800 million.

British people had 'never had it so good'

In 1957, Macmillan made his famous speech asserting the British people had 'never had it so good'. While this was largely true, much consumer spending was on credit, and, while employment remained high, unemployment was nevertheless growing – from 367,000 in 1951 to 563,000 by 1958.

'Stop–Go'

Conservative chancellors followed a policy of **'Stop–Go'**. This meant the use of interest rates to control economic growth. When the economy appeared to be growing too quickly, interest rates would be raised, making the cost of borrowing more expensive and reducing demand. When the economy slowed, however, interest rates would be cut, making credit cheaper and creating an increase in demand.

However, as elections approached budgets were manipulated to win more support. Hence in the 1959 budget, the Chancellor introduced tax cuts so people had more to spend – although he should have raised interest rates to reduce spending in the face of growing inflation.

Experts could increasingly see problems with the economy – indeed Macmillan's entire team of Treasury Ministers resigned in 1957 over 'Stop–Go' measures. They wanted to reduce government spending, for example, on welfare.

Planning economic growth

The government preferred to promote economic growth. In 1961 it set up two organisations to develop a planned economy:

- National Economic Development Council (NEDDY) in which representatives of employers, unions and government planned growth
- National Incomes Commission (NICKY) to regulate wage demands.

In July 1961, the Government announced a **'pay pause'** in the public sector to try to curb excessive pay demands throughout the economy. However, they gave in to demands from electricity workers who were threatening strikes, and the 'pay pause' was effectively a non-starter.

The economy in 1964

By the 1964 election, problems were more apparent. Unemployment had risen to 800,000 in 1963. Chancellor Reginald Maudling adopted a free-spending budget, reducing interest rates and cutting taxes to try to reduce the levels of unemployment. Although the measures saw unemployment fall to 500,000 by 1964, the budget deficit was £800 million. The Government had tried unsuccessfully to join the **European Economic Community,** which was enjoying growth rates far in excess of those in Britain (see page 18).

Identify relevant content

Examine Source A. Note down the content in the source that is relevant to answering the question below.

> With reference to these sources and your understanding of the historical context, which of these two sources is more valuable in explaining how far Britain was prosperous by the late 1950s?

SOURCE A

From Macmillan's 'Never had it so good' speech at Bedford, 20 July 1957, to Conservative supporters

Let's be frank about it: most of our people have never had it so good. Go around the country, go to the industrial towns, go to the farms and you will see a state of prosperity such as we have never had in my lifetime – nor indeed in the history of this country. What is worrying some of us is 'Is this too good to be true?' or perhaps I should say 'Is it too good to last?' For amid all this prosperity, there is one problem that has troubled us … It's the problem of rising prices. Our constant concern today is – can prices be steadied while at the same time we maintain full employment in an expanding economy. Can we control inflation? This is the problem of our time.

 Identify the significance of provenance

Now look at Source B. Still using the same question as in the first activity, comment on Source B's reliability. You should consider issues such as:
● who the author is and how authoritative she may be about the events she is describing
● when the source was produced and how distant it is from the events it describes
● the author's purpose.

SOURCE B

From Jennifer Worth, *Call the Midwife*, a memoir of a midwife working among the poorer classes in the East End of London in the 1950s; Worth was concerned that there were few accounts of the work of midwives in literature. The memoir was written in part to redress the balance.

By the 1950s most houses had running cold water and flushing lavatories in the yard outside. Some even had a bathroom. The tenements however did not, and the public wash-houses were still very much in use. Grumbling boys were taken there once a week to have a bath by determined mothers. The men, probably under female orders, carried out the same weekly ablution. You would see them going to the bath house on a Saturday afternoon with a small towel, a piece of soap, and a dour expression, which spoke of a weekly tussle once again waged and lost.

Most houses had a wireless but I did not see a single TV set during my time in the East End, which may have contributed to the size of the families.

Social and cultural developments

Rising living standards: the impact of affluence and consumerism

Living standards rose during the 1950s as never before for many sectors of society.

It was an age of consumerism, often fuelled by credit. Many bought items on hire purchase, with a deposit followed by weekly payments. Car ownership grew significantly from 3 to 7 million, and many could afford domestic appliances such as vacuum cleaners, washing machines, cookers and refrigerators for the first time. National television developed, with the number of sets growing from 340,000 in 1951 to 13 million by 1963. TV revolutionised many people's social lives as they preferred to stay at home and watch programmes rather than go out, for example, to the theatre or cinema.

The position of women

The 1950s is commonly seen as a regressive age for women, largely tied to the home and childcare. Career opportunities were often limited – for example, to light factory or clerical work.

- Most professional women became nurses, teachers or office workers.
- Women on average received 40 per cent less pay for doing the same jobs as men, although there were some changes – the civil service, for example, introduced equal pay in 1958.
- In schools, expectations of girls tended to be low, with some concentration on subjects such as domestic science to prepare girls for their anticipated role in life.
- Less than 2 per cent of women went to university during the 1950s.

Nevertheless there were changes afoot with, for example, Maureen Nicol beginning the National Housewives' Register to bring women closer together, and Dora Russell organising a **peace caravan** to protest against nuclear weapons. These women acted as role models for many who sought more than domesticity.

Class and the establishment

Britain was still seen as dominated by class. The Conservative government itself, composed largely of wealthy, privileged males, seemed to reflect the enduring power of the establishment. However, things were changing.

- The Second World War had seen some levelling of society and had engendered a sense of 'all being in it together'.
- The creation of the welfare state and the National Health Service under the Labour governments of 1945 to 1951 had led to significant improvements in well-being and raised the expectations of the less well-off.
- The growing affluence and improving living standards served to reduce class divisions to some extent.
- Satire and government scandals helped to encourage a decline in deference.

Cultural developments

One of the biggest cultural developments was the huge growth in television. The BBC had a monopoly of both radio and TV until 1956 when commercial television began with programmes financed by advertising. Most television was designed for escapism and entertainment but there were nevertheless high-quality dramas, usually performed live. In the theatre, meanwhile, a new social realism known as 'kitchen sink drama' began, with plays reflecting tensions in society rather than the comedies of manners to which audiences were used. Playwrights such as John Osborne were dubbed 'Angry Young Men'. Many of their works were filmed, bringing them to a wider audience, and indeed the genre was adapted for television in *Coronation Street*, which first appeared on screens in 1961.

Mind map

Use the information on the opposite page and your own knowledge to add detail to the mind map below to show the main social and cultural developments in the period 1951 to 1964.

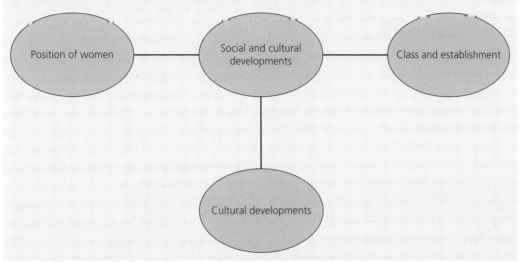

Position of women

Social and cultural developments

Class and establishment

Cultural developments

 ## Spectrum of importance

Below is a list of reasons why the 1950s is often regarded as a retrospective decade for women. Indicate their relative importance by writing their numbers on the spectrum and justify your placement, explaining why some factors are more important than others.

1 Women were expected to devote their lives to housework and raising children.

2 There were limited job opportunities for women.

3 Women received on average less pay than men.

4 Schools generally had low expectations of girls.

5 Men resented women who were assertive, for example, Dora Russell and her peace caravan.

6 Women were often isolated until the National Housewives' Register brought them into closer contact.

7 Many men thought of themselves as superior to women.

Least important   Most important

Social tensions

During the 1950s social tensions developed, particularly in the fields of race relations and attitudes to young people.

Race relations and attitudes to immigration

As labour shortages grew, people from the **New Commonwealth** – for example, India, Pakistan and the Caribbean – were encouraged to move to Britain mainly to work in unskilled or semi-skilled jobs.

- Asian communities often became centred in textile areas of northern towns.
- Areas of heavy industry such as the West Midlands attracted Asian and Caribbean communities.
- London became a magnet for all groups.

The new arrivals faced discrimination of various kinds, noticeably in housing.

Immigration into the UK (to the nearest 100,000)

Decade	Immigration
1940–49	240,000
1950–59	676,000
1960–69	1,243,000

Source: taken from M. Lynch, *Access to History: Britain 1945–2007*, page 55 (2008)

Racial violence

In 1958 there was a series of racial attacks in various cities from Nottingham to Notting Hill in London on August Bank Holiday. Initial television coverage showing attacks on the police and firefighters trying to douse burning buildings drew attention to the conflict and may have prompted further disturbances. The subsequent inquiry found tensions were largely the result of cultural differences and pressure on availability of accommodation. Inevitably immigration into already overcrowded and often deprived areas caused problems.

The Salmon Report

The Salmon Report was the official inquiry into the race riots. This found the following reasons for tensions.

- The indigenous population resented the willingness of immigrants to work for low wages, which they feared undercut their own employment potential.
- Immigrants were forcing up the cost of rents and were prepared to live in cramped conditions to share out the cost of accommodation, thus lessening the housing stock available to whites.
- There was some sexual jealousy: it was felt that immigrants, from the New Commonwealth, particularly from the Caribbean, were 'too attractive to many white women'.

Existing laws gave all Commonwealth citizens the right of citizenship and residence in Britain. In 1962 the Commonwealth Immigration Act limited immigration according to whether:

- would-be migrants had a job to go to
- they possessed particular skills, for example, in medicine
- they were dependants of people already here.

The emergence of the teenager and youth culture

The post-war years had seen large numbers of births – the so-called **baby boom**. By the 1950s these young people were growing up. The decade saw tensions between the generations. In an era of full employment, young people began to develop their own cultures through having disposable incomes at a relatively early age. While in most cases any 'rebellion' was limited to teenage fashions, and listening to rock and roll music, there was concern with the development of a specific youth group – Teddy Boys.

Teddy Boys

Teddy Boys were identified by slicked-back hair and Edwardian-style suits, but they also tended to show a lack of respect to older people and were feared by many as being violent. This was shown in gang fights (often against **conscripts** in military uniform), vandalism, particularly in dance halls and cinemas, and racist attacks on immigrants from the New Commonwealth.

! Delete as applicable

Below are a sample AS exam-style question and a paragraph written in answer to it. Read the paragraph and decide which of the possible options in bold is most appropriate. Delete the least applicable options and complete the paragraph by justifying your selection.

> 'The 1950s were a period of social tensions.' Explain why you agree or disagree with this view.

> The 1950s saw serious social tensions. There were, for example, instances of racial conflict culminating in inner-city riots in 1958. Immigrants from the New Commonwealth had been invited to Britain because of labour shortages but they often faced discrimination and hostility. Having said this, they were mainly concentrated in urban centres so racial conflict was not a national issue. The decade also saw generational conflict particularly in the growth of youth cultures such as Teddy Boys, who were widely accused of violence and vandalism. In fact, it was often Teddy Boys who were responsible for racial attacks and became involved in the 1958 race riots. While many teenagers often had disposable income, which they spent on fashions and music different from those favoured by older generations, most did not cause trouble and shared the same values as their parents. The 1950s **were / were partially / were not** a period of social tensions because ...

Identify the tone and emphasis of a source   a

Study Source A below. Don't focus on the content, but concentrate instead on:

- the language
- the sentence structure
- the emphasis of the source
- the overall tone.

What do the tone and emphasis of the source suggest about its value in terms of:

- the reliability of the evidence
- the utility of the evidence for studying attitudes towards immigrants from the New Commonwealth?

SOURCE A

From *Kensington News and West London Times*, 5 September 1958

As I turned into Bramley Road I saw a mob of over 700 men, women and children stretching 200 yards along the road. Young children of ten were treating the whole affair as a great joke and shouting, 'Come on let's get the blacks and the coppers. Let's get on with it.' In the middle of the screaming, jeering youths and adults a speaker from the Union Movement [a far right racist movement] was urging his excited audience to 'get rid of them' (the coloured people*) ...

Suddenly hundreds of leaflets were thrown into the crowd. A fierce cry rent the air and the mob rushed off in the direction of Latimer Road ... Women grabbed their children and chased after their menfolk. Dogs ran in among the crowd barking. Everywhere there was confusion ...

* These are the words of the far-right speaker.

Foreign policy: Europe, the Cold War and decolonisation

Foreign relations

Britain's overwhelming dilemma in the 1950s was that it sought to maintain a global influence but lacked the resources to do so. This was particularly evident during the development of the **Cold War** where Britain wanted its own nuclear deterrent. The result was that Britain was spending 8 per cent of its **gross domestic product (GDP)** on defence.

Relations with the USA and USSR

Britain was firmly tied to **NATO** (North Atlantic Treaty Organization) and the USA during the Cold War, becoming heavily involved, for example, in the Korean War (1950–53). Macmillan tried to act as a mediator between the superpowers, emphasising the 'special relationship' between Britain and the USA. He always supported the USA in disputes such as the 1962 Cuban Missile Crisis.

EFTA and attempts to join the European Economic Community (EEC)

Many felt Britain should look nearer to home and develop closer ties with Europe. The EEC had been founded in 1957 and was widely regarded as a huge success. Founder member West Germany, for example, achieved an average growth rate of more than 5 per cent between 1951 and 1964 compared with less than 2.5 per cent in Britain.

When the EEC was formed Britain showed little interest in joining. It had been involved in the formation of the European Free Trade Association (EFTA) as an alternative but this consisted mainly of smaller countries such as Norway and Austria with which it did comparatively little trade.

Britain's international interests

However, by the late 1950s Britain had changed policy and applied to join the EEC. This was vetoed by the French President, Charles de Gaulle. He feared Britain's commitment to Europe was too weak. He didn't want to see special trade agreements, for example, with the Commonwealth, and felt Britain was too close to the USA. De Gaulle used his veto again when Britain reapplied in 1965.

Polaris

In the 1961 application de Gaulle criticised Britain's failure to build nuclear weapons jointly with France while buying the Polaris system from the USA. While Britain still insisted on its own nuclear deterrent, this would never be large enough to give it real influence.

The 'Winds of Change' and decolonisation

The post-war period saw the demise of Britain's overseas empire through the granting of independence to the former colonies. While this was usually peaceful, it did face wars in Malaya and Kenya plus considerable unrest in Cyprus.

Beginning with Ghana in 1957, Britain gave independence to the majority of its colonies by 1968. Macmillan in particular recognised that colonialism was dead in his 'Winds of Change' speech in South Africa in 1960. He spoke of the right of peoples to govern themselves. This speech also resonated in neighbouring Rhodesia where a white supremacist government declared independence in 1965 rather than submit to majority black African rule.

The event that more than any other showed the impracticality of European countries forcing their will on others as part of a colonial policy was the Suez Crisis of 1956.

Suez Crisis 1956

Egypt's leader Gamal Abdul Nasser resented the fact that the **Suez Canal**, a major world waterway, was largely owned by British and French shareholders and brought little wealth to Egypt where it was sited. In 1956, Nasser nationalised the Canal. Britain and France made a secret agreement at Sèvres with Israel whereby Israel would invade Egypt, and Britain and France would invade the Canal Zone, ostensibly to keep the waterway open.

While the military campaign was successful it was opposed by the USA, the USSR and significant groups within Britain itself. The USA threatened to withdraw British loans if it did not withdraw its troops. Britain did withdraw. Prime Minister Anthony Eden resigned, and the Government was widely seen to have been humbled. It was this that showed Britain's reduced role in the world.

Judgements on the value of a source

Read Source A below along with the alternative answers that assess the value of the source in explaining how far Britain was united in the invasion of Suez in November 1956.

Which answer will gain the highest level in the mark scheme on page 7? Explain why.

> The source is valuable regarding how far Britain was united in its attitudes to the invasion of Suez because it tells you about the House of Commons debate so we know what the politicians were thinking. It shows that Labour was indecisive and the politicians weren't united.

> The source is unreliable because it is biased. The *Daily Telegraph* supported the Conservatives so made Labour look bad.

> The source is partially valuable in examining how far Britain was united in the invasion of Suez because it reflects the debates in Parliament and shows that Labour was indecisive. This suggests that the politicians at least were not united. However, the *Daily Telegraph*, a newspaper which normally supports the Conservatives, shows bias, which limits its reliability. It uses language such as 'pettiness', 'niggled' and 'haggled', which suggests Labour was more concerned with being obstructionist than adopting the united front that it clearly felt was necessary. The use of tone and language limits its utility as an objective indicator of divisions.

SOURCE A

From the *Daily Telegraph* report on the House of Commons debate on the Suez invasion, Tuesday, 30 October 1956; the *Daily Telegraph* generally supported the Conservative government. Labour MPs generally opposed the invasion.

It was a confused and anxious debate on the Egypt–Israel situation in the House of Commons tonight. Opposition speakers buzzed with anger but they could not make up their minds what they were angry about.

Apart from the figures of the division, a 270–218 defeat for the Socialists [the Labour Opposition], it was an easy win for the Government. The prime minister who had had to speak from what might be called early dawn to dewy eve carried his difficult bat …

Clumsiness and lack of statesmanship marked the resumption of the debate. Mr Gaitskell threw away all the opportunities which he had tried to create for the opposition earlier in the afternoon.

It was an occasion for showing both Parliament and the country that the opposition was able to transcend pettiness. But the Socialist leader niggled and haggled.

Recommended reading

- George L. Bernstein, *The Myth of Decline*, pages 54–63, 132–153 (2004)
- Peter Hennessy, *Having It So Good*, pages 405–490, 547–574 (2007)
- Dominic Sandbrook, *Never Had It So Good*, pages 31–147 (2005)

1 The Affluent Society 1951–64

Exam focus

Below is an AS level exam-style question and a high-level answer. Read the answer, annotations and comments to understand how it has been marked.

'The Conservative governments managed the economy effectively during the period 1951 to 1964.' Explain why you agree or disagree with this view.

Britain seemed to enjoy unparalleled prosperity during the 1950s. Unemployment remained low and there were huge growths in living standards. However, prosperity was not universal across the country. Some areas remained poor, and housing conditions squalid. Nevertheless for those in work it was a consumer age, with the growth of household goods and television sets and motor cars, often paid for with credit.

Introduction shows question focus is well understood.

Much of the prosperity was attributed to effective economic management by the Conservative governments. However, there was little disagreement on broad issues between the two major parties – to the extent that economic policies were known as 'Butskellism', an amalgam of the names of R.A. Butler and Hugh Gaitskell, the Conservative and Labour politicians most responsible for economic affairs during the early 1950s. Economic aims included the maintenance of full employment and economic growth, the continued development of the welfare state as an insurance for the most vulnerable members of society and, in terms of the National Health Service, to keep the nation fit and well so that working days were not lost to absence through preventable illness. Both parties moreover supported defence commitments and the development of nuclear weapons, which they felt enabled Britain to remain as a world power. This did, however, lead to too many commitments. Britain, for example, could not remain as a major world power with global commitments as well as provide a comprehensive welfare system and increase economic growth. Indeed there was a growing balance of payments deficit as Britain imported more than it sold abroad.

Evidence of continuity and change.

Identification of a key problem.

One problem was inflation; indeed people spoke of stagflation – prices rising despite the economy contracting. Unemployment was nevertheless growing – from 367,000 in 1951 to 563,000 by 1958. When Harold Macmillan made his famous 'Never had it so good' speech in Bedford in July 1957 in fact he was warning his audience against complacency, fearing that rising prices was Britain's biggest economic problem and could threaten the prosperity that so many enjoyed. The entire team of Treasury Ministers in fact resigned in 1958 over 'Stop-Go' policies. They felt the Government should be cutting back expenditure and retrenching in order to reduce inflation. Inflation moreover led to excessive pay claims to maintain living standards. While Britain may not have been as 'strike prone' as it was to prove in future decades, the signs were there.

Useful evidence in support.

Striking a balance in terms of the question.

Overall however the biggest issue was the growing balance of payments deficit. It rose from £540 million in 1957 to £800 million by 1964. Governments tried to alleviate this by 'Stop-Go' policies. Interest rates were deployed to control economic growth. When the economy showed signs of overheating or growing too quickly, interest rates would be raised, to make the cost of borrowing more expensive. This reduced demand for goods and the economy slowed. If it slowed too much, interest rates would be lowered, thus making the cost of borrowing cheaper and increasing demand, thereby stimulating growth.

Judgement supported by valid evidence.

Governments realised, however, that the illusion of prosperity increased their popularity. Therefore, as elections approached they often used budgets to lower interest rates or introduce tax cuts, to give people more disposable income – even if this went against prevailing economic circumstances.

Hence in the 1959 budget, the Chancellor introduced tax cuts so people had more to spend – although he should have raised interest rates to reduce spending in the face of growing inflation. Chancellor Reginald Maudling in particular was guilty of this in his 1963 budget when he reduced taxes and interest rates to try to stimulate growth.

By the late 1950s moreover economic problems were becoming more evident. The Government hoped to stimulate growth, through the maintenance of trust in a planned economy. To this end it set up in 1961 two organisations to develop a planned economy: the National Economic Development Council (NEDDY) in which representatives of employers, unions and government planned growth, and the National Incomes Commission (NICKY) to regulate wage demands. However in July 1961, the government announced a 'pay pause' in the public sector to try to curb excessive pay demands throughout the economy. Nevertheless they gave in to demands from electricity workers who were threatening strikes, and the 'pay pause' was effectively a non-starter.

It will be seen therefore that while on the surface the British economy appeared successful during the period 1951 to 1964, problems increasingly emerged. While the main parties were in broad agreement as to economic policy based on growth and the maintenance of welfare and defence commitments, some policies such as 'Stop-Go' may not have been as efficient as desired. Economic difficulties moreover were compounded by using budgets as bribes to electors as elections approached when the policy of tax reductions, for example, may not have been in the economic interest. While the two main problems may have been growing inflation and the balance of payment deficits, these were not addressed effectively as the period developed.

Conclusion summarises effectively in order to arrive at a judgement.

This is an excellent AS essay, attaining Level 5. It is cogent, well argued and structured, with a range of clear information addressing the issues. There is some discussion of continuity and change, notably in the second paragraph. Overall the range of the question is well understood, and the concluding judgement is soundly based on what has been argued in the essay.

Reverse engineering

The best essays are based on careful plans. Read the essay and the examiner's comments and try to work out the general points of the plan used to write the essay. Once you have done this, note down the specific examples used to support each general point.

Exam focus

Below is a sample high-level answer to an A-level exam-style question. Read it and the comments around it.

'Foreign policy in the period 1951 to 1964 was dominated by the desire to maintain a global influence.' Assess the validity of this view.

Britain's foreign policy was dominated in large part by a desire to retain its global influence, although this was threatened in the period 1951 to 1964. It sought to maintain its global influence through the development of nuclear weapons, which gave it superpower status, and commitments across the world. However, it increasingly lacked the resources to do so. The example of Suez moreover showed that Britain could no longer dictate to developing nations and sent a clear message that its global status was in fact over. Having said this, Prime Minister Harold Macmillan recognised the world was changing and imperialism was a spent force, as exemplified by his 'Winds of Change' speech in South Africa in 1960, and Britain was trying to give independence to former countries of the Empire as peacefully and effectively as possible. It did therefore recognise that developed nations could no longer dictate to or govern less developed ones.

> Strong, focused introduction outlines question parameters.

Britain lacked the resources to maintain superpower status although it tried to do so throughout the period 1951 to 1964: indeed over 8 per cent of the national budget went on defence during this period. Britain not only sought the nuclear deterrent but also attempted to meet global commitments through large-scale conventional forces. However, it was the Suez Crisis of 1956 that brought home the reality of its limitations on the global stage.

> Attempts to strike a balance.

> Link to next paragraph.

The Suez Canal, a major world waterway that lay in Egypt, was owned by British and French shareholders. In 1956 President Nasser nationalised the Canal to pay for his own ambitious projects. The lease of the Canal only had thirteen years to run so Britain and France would eventually relinquish control of the Canal anyway, but their leaders decided Nasser must not be allowed to get away with this action. They therefore did a deal with Egypt's enemy, Israel, whereby Israel would attack Egypt and British and French forces invade the Canal Zone ostensibly to protect the Canal but in fact to win back control. Militarily the invasion succeeded – but Britain in particular was forced to withdraw. Neither superpower supported the action. That the USSR might have threatened retaliation was expected, but the USA too opposed the invasion and indeed threatened to withdraw loans if Britain didn't withdraw. Given its dependence on US finance, Britain was in no position to continue its actions in Suez.

> Possibly rather a narrative paragraph and could be more clearly focused on the question.

However, the subsequent withdrawal was widely seen as a humiliation by other developing countries. It led to sweeping defence cuts in Britain of conventional forces and a focus on nuclear weapons. Even here, however, Britain's ambitions were limited because of the cost. Indeed, with Britain relying on the Polaris system bought from the USA, it attracted the criticism of France for not helping to develop a joint UK–French system. While Britain insisted on an independent nuclear deterrent, it was in fact largely dependent on the USA.

> Return to question focus.

In diplomatic terms, while Macmillan in particular tried to act as a mediator between the USA and USSR in international disputes, Britain's influence was limited. Macmillan may have been consulted but he was not a prime mover in events.

> This section could be developed – tending to assertion.

Global influence can be measured in a variety of ways. While it may imply superpower status, it could also reflect moral leadership. The period 1951 to 1964 was one of decolonisation, with the former colony of Ghana gaining independence in 1957 and others following. Britain did try to prepare colonies for independence, although the process was not without bloodshed, as evidenced by the insurgencies in Malaya and Kenya. Cyprus also provided a problem in the conflict between

ENOSIS, which sought union with Greece, and the British authorities. Macmillan in particular however may have wanted Britain to act as a model in the decolonisation process, as evidenced by his Winds of Change speech in South Africa where he asserted that different peoples had the right to govern themselves and colonisation was effectively a thing of the past. Certainly Britain did not cling aggressively to colonies and genuinely tried to manage a peaceful transition.

> Again this could be more focused on the question.

It may be, however, that it was Britain's relationship with the EEC that got to the heart of its continuing desire for global influence. When the EEC was instituted after the Treaty of Rome in 1957, Britain was largely indifferent. It saw itself in a tripartite relationship in terms of foreign affairs – with Europe on the one hand but also closely tied to the Commonwealth and the USA. It did not therefore wish to overemphasise its relationship with Europe at the expense of the other two – even if a close relationship with the USA was in part illusionary – as we have seen, the USA, for example, had opposed Britain during the Suez Crisis. This ambivalence in terms of Britain's ties to Europe was also noted by President de Gaulle of France. When Britain did actually apply to join in 1961, de Gaulle vetoed the application, questioning Britain's commitment to Europe and also what he believed was its close relationship with the USA, which would bring undue US influence into the EEC.

> Explains Britain's dilemma concerning involvement in Europe well.

Britain certainly hoped to remain a global player, but the cost of maintaining commitments and building nuclear weapons precluded this. While it may have retained influence with the USA, it was nevertheless not a prime mover in international crises involving the superpowers during the period. The example of the Suez Crisis came as a shock where Britain was humiliated largely as a result of US opposition to its actions. Britain believed its foreign relations were wider than Europe, which is why it was indifferent to the original inception of the EEC, seeing a balance of interests between Europe, the USA and the Commonwealth played out necessarily on a global scale. Nevertheless Britain also felt it had a moral influence globally through, for example, its largely honourable policy of decolonisation. However, Suez showed Britain's limitations on the global scale without US support and the costs of global commitments were too high to maintain. Indeed during this period, Britain may have learned the harsh lesson that it was no longer a global superpower, but it still could exert global influence through other means.

> Conclusion returns to question focus and makes a valid judgement.

This essay begins well and clearly understands the key issues, but does stray occasionally into narrative in which the focus is less central. There is probably enough particularly in the introduction, Europe sections and conclusion to have elements of Level 5, but it might be more likely to remain overall in high Level 4. It is well organised with useful information in support but as it stands it is not fully analytical.

Moving from a Level 4 to Level 5

The A-level exam focus essay at the end of Section 3 (pages 58–59) provides a Level 5 essay. The essay here achieves a Level 4. Read both essays, and the comments provided. Make a list of the additional features required to push a Level 4 essay into Level 5.

Harold Wilson and the Labour governments

REVISED

Political developments 1964–75

The Labour government began its work in 1964 full of the optimism of the 1960s, committed to modernisation, liberalisation and the development of science and technology. It was noted for liberal reforms such as the abolition of the death penalty and legalisation of abortion but was less successful in managing the economy.

Political leaders

- Harold Wilson, the prime minister, was from a lower middle class background, had excelled at Oxford and served as a senior civil servant during the war. Wilson was highly regarded in terms of organisational ability but many considered him untrustworthy as a politician, and he in turn tended to detect conspiracies among colleagues. This limited his effectiveness as a leader.
- Roy Jenkins was to become one of the most reforming of Home Secretaries, overseeing the legalisation of abortion and homosexuality, liberalising divorce laws and overseeing the final abolition of the death penalty.
- James Callaghan who had risen through the trade union movement served as Jenkins' successor as Home Secretary, having earlier been Chancellor of the Exchequer.

In the 1970 general election, the Conservatives were returned to power under their leader Edward Heath.

The economy 1964–73

The economy came to dominate British politics from the mid-1960s. Wilson inherited a deficit of £800 million and foreigners were increasingly reluctant to invest in **sterling**. The priority was to rebuild the British economy and increase exports to pay off this deficit and thereby raise international confidence in sterling. This Government was committed to achieving this through central planning.

Department of Economic Affairs

A new Department of Economic Affairs was created under Minister George Brown. Its aim was to create a National Plan to guide economic development by encouraging competition between government, employers and trade unions – for example, members of the **Trades Union Congress (TUC)**. However, economic growth remained poor and by 1967 the Plan was dropped.

While Wilson won a second term of office in 1966, economic problems mounted.

- Industrial disputes proliferated often at a local level. **Local shop stewards** called unofficial or 'wildcat' strikes often by a show of hands. Britain lost over 3 million working days to strikes in 1960 and 10 million in 1970. An extensive seamen's strike in 1966 and the dockers' strike of 1967 were both particularly damaging as they reduced exports.
- Sterling, valued too highly, was in a continuous crisis. In November 1967 the Government devalued sterling by 14 per cent from £1 = US$2.80 to £1 = US$2.40. This improved exports, which became cheaper, but led to greater inflation at home as imports became more expensive; by 1968 inflation had risen to 18 per cent per annum.
- Although unemployment remained low at less than 2 per cent, it was slowly growing.

Balance of payments deficits (in £ millions)

Year	Deficit
1961	−95
1964	−382
1967	−301

▲ Source: Pollard British Economy 1914–1990, page 307, taken from George L. Bernstein, *The Myth of Decline*, page 181, Pimlico (2004)

The 1970 election

The Conservatives were rather surprising winners in the 1970 election, with an overall majority of 30 seats. The reasons were a combination of failures by Labour and successful tactics by the Conservatives.

Failures of Labour

Wilson's government had an unsuccessful economic record, with rising unemployment and inflation. In addition it had failed to join the EEC for a second time, and had been defeated by the trade unions on its industrial relations policies.

Conservative success

The Conservatives had campaigned well, promising trade union reform and less government interference in the economy. The party offered a 'new style of government' to which many, especially members of the growing middle classes, seemed receptive.

Identify the tone and emphasis of a source   **a**

Study Source A below. Don't focus on the content, but concentrate instead on:

- the language
- the sentence structure
- the emphasis of the source
- the overall tone.

What does the tone and emphasis of the source suggest about its value in terms of:

- the reliability of the evidence
- the utility of the evidence in studying the impact of devaluation?

SOURCE A

Harold Wilson explains the impact of devaluation; taken from a transcript of a BBC broadcast to the nation by Harold Wilson on 19 November 1967

Tonight we must face the new situation. First, what this means. From now the pound abroad is worth 14 per cent or so less in terms of other currencies. This does not mean, of course, that the pound here in Britain, in your pocket or purse or in your bank, has been devalued. What it does mean is that we shall now be able to sell more goods abroad on a competitive basis. This is a tremendous opportunity for all our exporters, and for many who have not yet started to sell their goods overseas. But it will also mean that the goods that we buy from abroad will be dearer and so for many of these goods it will be cheaper to buy British.

 Support or challenge

Below is a sample exam-style question that asks you how far you agree with a specific statement. Beneath that is a series of general statements that are relevant to the question. Using your own knowledge and the information on the opposite page, decide whether these statements support or challenge the statement in the question.

How far do you agree that Labour faced significant economic problems during its period of office from 1964 to 1970?

	Support	Challenge
Labour inherited a deficit of £800 million.		
The Department of Economic Affairs was given the task of producing a plan for economic growth.		
British industry was beset with industrial disputes.		
The Government devalued the currency in 1967 and exports grew.		
Economic growth remained poor.		
Unemployment remained low.		
Inflation was growing to 18 per cent per annum by 1968.		

Problems for the Labour government

Two of the most serious problems for the Labour government were:
- poor industrial relations, which significantly disrupted production
- the beginnings of the Troubles in Northern Ireland.

Industrial relations

The Labour Party traditionally had a strong relationship with trade unions, which largely funded it. However, this did not necessarily mean the union movement worked in harmony with it. The 1960s saw significant industrial unrest including a damaging seamen's strike in 1966. A Prices and Incomes Freeze in 1966 failed as unions struck for higher pay.

'In Place of Strife'

Determined to tackle the issue, the government produced a **White Paper**, 'In Place of Strife', in 1969. This advocated restrictions on the right to strike – a proper ballot should be held, for example, instead of a show of hands, and there should be a 28-day **'cooling-off period'** to give time for a settlement to be reached. Employers meanwhile would have to honour agreements and agree to consult with trade unions about any changes in working practices.

The White Paper split the government, with Home Secretary James Callaghan in particular opposing the proposals. Trade unions meanwhile refused to co-operate and even threatened to cut their funding to the Labour Party if the proposals went ahead. The White Paper was abandoned and the absence of any real policy on labour relations was a determinant factor in Labour's electoral defeat in 1970.

Beginnings of the Troubles in Northern Ireland

Background

Northern Ireland, often referred to as Ulster, remained in the United Kingdom after the 1921 settlement while the rest of the island of Ireland formed the independent Irish Republic. Ulster had its own parliament at Stormont which took responsibility for domestic affairs; it was dominated by Protestants who gerrymandered elections to ensure they remained the majority. Ulster's Catholic minority faced discrimination noticeably in jobs and housing while the **Royal Ulster Constabulary**, particularly the part-time 'B specials', were seen by many Catholics as an organisation of repression. Although the province had largely remained peaceful during the post-war period, by the late 1960s tensions were mounting and violence was increasing.

Breakdown of order

As Catholics demanded more civil rights in the late 1960s, their marches and protests frequently came under attack from Protestants. After a particularly serious outbreak of disorder in the Bogside area of Londonderry in August 1969, the Labour government sent in troops to restore order. The Provisional IRA was formed to force the British to relinquish their control of the province. They saw the British as a colonial power and felt if they could be forced to leave, a settlement could be reached with the Protestants. However, they were opposed by Protestant Ulster Unionists who formed their own paramilitary organisations such as the Ulster Defence Association (UDA) and Ulster Volunteer Force (UVF). By the early 1970s the province was effectively in the grip of civil war.

Mind map

Use the information on the opposite page and your own knowledge to add detail to the mind map below to show the main political developments in the years 1964–70.

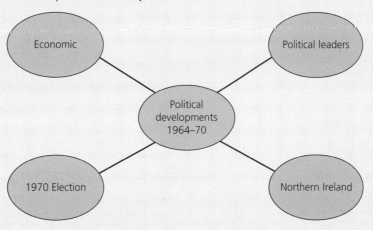

Eliminate irrelevance

Below is an A-level question and part of the answer. Identify those parts of the answer that are relevant. Draw a line through the information that is not relevant.

To what extent were poor industrial relations responsible for the problems the Labour government of 1964 to 1970 faced in successfully addressing economic problems?

The Labour Party won the 1964 election by a narrow margin of four seats. It was committed to modernising Britain through the 'white heat' of technology. However, although problems in the economy came to dominate much government thinking during the period 1964 to 1970, the Labour government appeared not to address them particularly successfully. The first major development, for example, the creation of a Department of Economic Affairs, responsible for planning economic growth, appeared not well thought through and was closed down in 1969. It had endured a difficult relationship with the Treasury with which its responsibilities overlapped.

One perennial problem was the refusal of trade unions to co-operate in wage restraint. Even though the TUC was involved in the creation of the National Plan, industrial action proliferated. British government had favoured centralised planning since the Second World War and much of British industry had been nationalised. However, by 1970 Britain was losing 10 million working days in strikes. The TUC and indeed some senior Labour leaders had scuppered In Place of Strife, while the seamen's strike of 1966 had harmed the exports on which Britain depended for economic growth. Of course industrial relations were not the only problem in the economy — the overvaluation of sterling led to a 14 per cent devaluation in 1968, for example, which may have stimulated cheaper exports but also helped fuel inflation. Nevertheless the lack of co-operation among trade unions remained a significant reason for the problems faced by the Labour government in addressing economic problems successfully and could in part account for the fact that they appeared not to have done so.

Liberal reforming legislation

Liberal reforms

Home Secretary Roy Jenkins has been equally praised and vilified for various pieces of legislation passed during his term of office (1965–67) which liberalised Britain. Much of the legislation, however, emanated either from **private members' bills**, which he supported, or was already in progress.

Race Relations Acts 1965 and 1968

These prohibited racial discrimination so, for example, a landlord could no longer refuse to rent accommodation to non-white people; a Race Relations Board to police this was set up while a Community Relations Commission attempted to improve relations between people of different ethnic groups. They did however conflict with the 1968 Commonwealth Immigration Act (see page 34).

Abortion Act 1967

Abortion had been illegal in Britain and figures as to its practice vary from 100,000 to 250,000 per year. However, it is known that 35,000 more wealthy women could undergo abortions in relatively safe conditions in private clinics in the care of professional medical personnel while the vast majority underwent 'backstreet abortions' in often insanitary environments with considerable risk. Liberal MP David Steel introduced the bill, which allowed legal termination where two doctors certified that continued pregnancy could lead to health risks for the mother.

Sexual Offences Act 1967

Introduced as a private member's bill by Labour MP Leo Abse, this legalised homosexual acts between consenting adults – although at eighteen the age of consent was higher than for heterosexuals.

Theatres Act 1968

This was a private member's bill introduced by Labour MP George Strauss which ended the right of a court official, the Lord Chamberlain, to censor theatre productions and saw the emergence of controversial plays and musicals in London's West End such as *Hair*, which showed full nudity on stage.

Divorce Reform Act 1969

This made divorce easier for couples who were living apart. It introduced the idea of 'no-guilt' divorce whereas before evidence of cruelty, desertion or adultery had to be shown. As a result the divorce rate shot up.

Abolition of the death penalty 1969

The death penalty had not operated for some years and its abolition was introduced as a four-year trial in 1965; it was made permanent in 1969.

Education reform

Secondary education had been based, since the 1944 Education Act, on a three-school system, and pupils took an 11-Plus exam to determine which school they should attend.
- Grammar schools catered for the brightest and gave them an academic education to prepare them for professional careers or universities.
- Technical schools catered for pupils who would benefit from a technical education – to prepare them, for example, for careers in engineering, technology or science.
- Secondary Modern schools were vocational-based schools for the majority of pupils.

In practice, few technical schools were built and many secondary moderns offered a very limited education. While grammar schools undoubtedly benefited many bright working class children the system was felt to be elitist. The answer lay in comprehensive schools where children of all abilities and from all backgrounds studied in the same school. In Circular 10/65 the Government encouraged the closure of selective schools and the opening of comprehensives to encourage equality of educational opportunity.

Compare two sources

Sources A and B give different views on the introduction of comprehensive education in 1965.

	Main points of content
Source A	
Source B	
Main similarities and differences	

You should now compare the two sources for provenance.

	Provenance in terms of Who? What? When?
Source A	
Source B	
Comments on provenance	

Having done this, you could compare the sources in terms of tone, language and emphasis.

	Tone, language, emphasis
Source A	
Source B	
Comments on similarities/differences in terms of tone language and emphasis	

When you have completed this activity, you should attempt the following AS-level exam-style question:

> With reference to these sources and your understanding of the historical context, which of these two sources is more valuable in explaining why the Government sought to introduce comprehensive education in the period 1964 to 1970?

SOURCE A

From Circular 10/65, the Circular sent by the Government to Local Authorities requesting them to submit plans to reorganise secondary education to create comprehensive schools

Introduction

It is the Government's declared objective to end the selection at eleven plus and to eliminate separatism in secondary education.

The Secretary of State accordingly requests local education authorities, if they have not already done so, to prepare and submit to him plans for reorganising secondary education in their areas on comprehensive lines ...

The School Community

The Secretary of State ... urges authorities to ensure, when determining catchment areas, that schools are as socially and intellectually comprehensive as is practicable ...

SOURCE B

From Brian Lapping, *The Labour Government 1964–1970*; Lapping is a well-respected political journalist and documentary maker

The rigid division of the population at the age of eleven into those selected for grammar schools and those rejected created unnecessary tension and fear among parents and children before examination and resentment afterwards ...

[A]s is so often the case with social reforms, the government's announcements and its statistics may give an exaggerated impression of the changes that actually occurred. The fact that the decisive government action in forwarding the introduction of comprehensive schools was a Circular from the Education Minister rather than an order or Act of parliament explains part of the difficulty. The central government was not legally responsible for providing schools ... the government could not give orders to the local authorities. All it could do was persuade and bribe them.

Social and cultural change

Teenagers

By the 1960s **baby boomers** had jobs and provided a new market in terms of films, music and the latest fashions or gadgets such as transistor radios. Television too produced shows for teenagers in general such as *Top of the Pops*, which began in January 1964, and at the same time targeted specific youth cultures, with programmes such as *Ready Steady Go!*, which was aimed at mods.

Youth culture and the 'permissive society'

Different teenage groups came and went in the 1960s. By the early 1960s, Teddy Boys were replaced by 'rockers'. Others became 'mods' riding sleek Vespa or Lambretta motor scooters from Italy. As the 1960s progressed, mods morphed into skinheads with short hair, braces and a working class arrogance, listening to reggae and ska-inspired music.

Youth cults had two things in common.
● Their proponents wanted to be noticed, perhaps to shock their elders.
● They were exploited by successful businesspeople who created their styles and then marketed them very successfully.

Some young people became hippies or supported an alternative culture, often rejecting societal values of materialism. For the vast majority, however, youth rebellion was a temporary phase before settling down to marriage and children. Most young people remained just as conservative as their parents.

Young people and violence

There was widespread concern about the apparent predilection of young people for violence. In May 1964 gangs of mods and rockers fought each other at seaside resorts. There were 51 arrests in Margate and 76 in Brighton. This shocked visitors who inevitably felt threatened in the disorder. The situation grew worse still with the widespread outbreaks of football violence particularly among gangs of skinheads which lasted into the 1980s and beyond. Many academics tried to explain the phenomenon in terms of disadvantaged youth or animal behaviour of territorial attack and defence, but the hooligans themselves tended to say they indulged in the violence simply because it was exciting and they enjoyed it.

It should be remembered that most young people were not violent and simply wanted to 'hang out' with the friends with whom they shared common interests. Indeed in 1945 the various Scouting movements including Girl Guides, Cubs and Brownies claimed 471,000 members; by 1970, admittedly after the baby boom, this had risen to 539,340.

The Swinging Sixties and the growth of the mass media

The 1960s seemed to open a cultural renaissance in Britain, very much focused on London. Britain had become a world leader in popular music driven by bands such as the Beatles and Rolling Stones, but it also led the way in such fields as photography, design and fashion. This was widely covered in the mass media, with a growth in TV and radio programmes and magazines aimed at youth, especially in terms of music and fashion.

The 'permissive society'

The so-called '**permissive society**' referred to a sense of greater freedom of behaviour, and less inhibition. More people considered themselves 'hip' and 'chic' and achieved celebrity status in a wide range of roles. Twiggy, for example, became the first 'superstar' model while photographers such as David Bailey and Terence Donovan were much in demand.

However, it must be remembered that the 'Swinging Sixties' bypassed most places in Britain, and the vast majority were more familiar with its music than any other aspect.

Support or challenge

Below is a sample exam-style question that asks how far you agree with a specific statement. Beneath that is a series of general statements that are relevant to the question. Using your own knowledge and the information on the opposite page, decide whether these statements support or challenge the statement in the question.

How significant were changes in culture during the 1960s?

	Support	Challenge
The 1960s saw a massive creativity in popular music.		
Britain was a world leader in photography, design and fashion.		
Cultural changes were largely focused on London.		
The 1960s saw the birth of celebrity, for example, in models and photographers.		
Except for popular music, the cultural changes bypassed most of Britain.		

 Eliminate irrelevance **a**

Below are a sample exam-style question and a paragraph written in answer to the question. Read the paragraph and identity those parts that are not directly related to the question. Draw a line through the information that is irrelevant and justify your deletions in the margin.

'Rebellious behaviour among young people was widespread in the 1960s.' Explain why you agree or disagree with this statement.

The 1960s was a period seen by many historians as a period of youth rebellion. Most young people had jobs and plentiful sources of income. They spent much of this on goods specifically targeted at their market. Many older people saw their appearance and musical tastes as a sign of rebellion. This was exacerbated by challenging behaviour such as violence in seaside resorts and, later in the decade, football hooliganism. Seeing violence was threatening to the older generation especially when young people themselves couldn't explain it beyond the thrill it gave them. However, most young people weren't in gangs and didn't indulge in violence. Even fewer became hippies espousing alternative lifestyles. It was however a period of celebrity among young people such as the model Twiggy and photographer David Bailey. These did become role models along with pop idols such as the Beatles and the Rolling Stones who enjoyed great success. Most youth cults were a phase and most young people remained as conservative as their parents. Indeed most favoured traditional clubs and activities such as the Scouting movement, which saw its membership grow from 471,000 members in 1945 to 539,340 by 1970.

Progress towards female equality

The 1960s saw the development of female protest movements. However, women were too diverse as a group, with different primary agendas, to be able to act effectively in concert.

Women in politics

The 1960s saw comparatively few developments in terms of women in politics. In the 1966 election fewer than 80 women stood for election and only 21 were successful. Few were promoted to high office. One exception, Barbara Castle, supported the Dagenham strikers (see below) but was reticent about female issues. A leading Conservative, Margaret Thatcher, gave no noticeable encouragement to other women to enter politics.

Second-wave feminism

Second-wave feminism grew as a movement to address concerns such as gender stereotyping, limited employment opportunities for women, and the demand for a greater role in society than childcare and household responsibilities. It was also known as 'women's liberation'.

Particularly significant was the demand for equal pay.

The Dagenham sewing machinists' strike of 1968

In 1968 management at the Ford Motor Company's car factory at Dagenham decided to pay the female sewing machinists who made car seat covers 15 per cent less in wages than men doing equivalent jobs. The female machinists went on strike for three weeks and the Secretary of State for Employment and Productivity, Barbara Castle, intervened in the dispute. She and the strikers negotiated a pay deal that increased wages by 7 per cent. The long-term impact of the strike was that it significantly raised the profile of the issue of unequal pay and was one of the main causes of the passing of the Equal Pay Act in 1970.

Women's liberation

It was protests such as the Dagenham strike that stimulated the women's liberation movement in Britain. Women had been voicing their frustrations with lack of career opportunities and the burden of domestic responsibilities since the 1940s, but little progress had been made. In the 1960s, some began to see the struggle for economic equality in terms of social inequalities, that women were treated as second-class citizens. Feminists organised a National Women's Conference in Oxford in 1970 which stimulated local groups to campaign and protest.

This coincided with growing high-profile activism such as marches and demonstrations including the attack on the Miss World contest in 1970 shown live on television.

Feminist literature

The late 1960s saw a profusion of feminist literature, from magazines such as *Shrew* to Germaine Greer's book *The Female Eunuch*, which received wide publicity. Greer argued that men's control over women had stifled their individuality and development.

Problems with the women's liberation movement

One problem with the feminist movement was that it covered so many diverse agendas, from wives who simply wanted more respect from their husbands to radical feminists who saw men as the enemy. It was difficult in these circumstances for concerted action to take place. Some did join female-only communes; others concentrated on economic issues, while still others prioritised issues such as abortion and birth control. The National Abortion Campaign, for example, was founded in 1975 to argue for extending the provisions of the 1967 Act (see page 28).

Others meanwhile, such as **'clean-up' campaigner** Mary Whitehouse, promoted the role of women as housemakers and mothers, often within the context of traditional family values and moral conduct. These campaigns received wide publicity.

Identify the tone and emphasis of a source a

Study Source A below. Don't focus on the content, but concentrate instead on:

- the language
- the sentence structure
- the emphasis of the source
- the overall tone.

What does the tone and emphasis of the source suggest about its value in terms of:

- the reliability of evidence
- the utility of the evidence for studying the motives behind second-wave feminism?

SOURCE A

An extract from Germaine Greer, *The Female Eunuch*, first published in 1970; Greer is a feminist writer whose views on the role and status of women have been hugely influential

[N]ow ungenteel middle-class women are calling for revolution. For many of them the call for revolution came before the call for the liberation of women …

The difference is radical, for the faith that the suffragettes had in the existing political systems and their deep desire to participate in them have perished. In the old days, ladies were anxious to point out that they did not seek to disrupt society or to unseat God. Marriage, the family, private property and the state were threatened by their actions, but they were anxious to allay the fears of conservatives, and in doing so the suffragettes betrayed their own cause and prepared the way for the failure of emancipation.

Five years ago it seemed clear that emancipation had failed: the number of women in Parliament had settled at a low level; the number of professional women had stabilized as a tiny minority; the pattern of female employment had emerged as underpaid, menial and supportive. The cage door had been opened but the canary had refused to fly out. The conclusion was that the cage door ought never to have been opened because canaries are made for captivity; the suggestion of an alternative had only confused and saddened them.

 Support or challenge

Below is a sample A-level exam-style question about the role and status of women during the 1960s. Beneath that is a series of general statements that are relevant to the question. Using your own knowledge and the information on the opposite page, decide whether or not these statements support or challenge the statement in the question.

'The role and status of women improved significantly during the 1960s.' How far do you agree with this statement?

	Support	Challenge
Many people saw women's role mainly in terms of home making and childcare.		
The 1960s saw women still having limited employment opportunities particularly in management positions.		
Girls faced inequalities at school, for example, low expectations in terms of career options.		
Women still faced unequal pay.		
The 1968 Dagenham sewing machinists' strike was a significant stepping stone on the road to equal pay. It involved the intervention of the Secretary of State for Employment and Productivity, Barbara Castle, one of the few women in government.		
While the Dagenham sewing machinists were awarded a seven per cent pay rise, they didn't get equal pay.		
Second-wave feminism was beginning to address more general concerns such as society's expectations of women, for example, their dominant role in housework and childcare, limited expectations in schools, and feminist issues such as gender stereotyping.		

Immigration and racial tensions

Racial tensions

Continued immigration led to racial tensions during the 1960s. This was apparent, for example, during an election in the West Midlands constituency of Smethwick in 1964 where the Conservative candidate adopted an overtly racist campaign. Immigrants from the **New Commonwealth** continued to face discrimination and sometimes attack despite legislation to prevent this. By 1968, the situation seemed to have worsened, partly due to the expulsion of Asian citizens from the former African colony of Kenya who sought, as was their legal right, sanctuary in the UK.

Kenyan Asians and the 1968 Commonwealth Immigration Act

By spring 1968, 2,000 Kenyan Asians were arriving in Britain each month. While they were known to be hard working and entrepreneurial, many people were hostile to their arrival. Home Secretary James Callaghan acknowledged these concerns with the 1968 Commonwealth Immigration Act.

Commonwealth Immigration Act

This Act tightened immigration rules.
- Children of migrants living in Britain were denied entry if they were over seventeen years of age.
- Children with only one parent living in Britain were denied entry.
- Entrants had to prove that parents of godparents were living in Britain.

Critics saw this legislation as very divisive and unfair. Indeed it restricted immigration from the New Commonwealth to 1,500 per year and left 200,000 Kenyan Asians adrift. Opinion polls however showed over 72 per cent of respondents were in support.

White backlash and the 'Rivers of Blood' speech

Despite the Commonwealth Immigration Act, continued immigration led to a **'white backlash'**. Shadow Defence Secretary Enoch Powell made his notorious 'Rivers of Blood' speech at Birmingham in April 1968 in which he argued that to prevent race war coloured immigrants should be encouraged to return home. Specifically he said:
- mass immigration and anti-racist laws meant immigrants had more rights than the indigenous white population
- multi-culturalism would lead to greater segregation rather than integration
- the Government should offer grants to non-white immigrants to return home.

Powell's speech resonated widely among whites, with 1,000 London dockers, for example, marching in support. He received thousands of letters approving his comments. Polls showed over 70 per cent supported his ideas.

Ironically the same government which tightened immigration was responsible for the passing of legislation to outlaw discrimination.

Legislation outlawing discrimination

Race Relations Acts 1965 and 1968

These two Acts together:
- outlawed racial discrimination in public places
- outlawed incitement to racial hatred
- set up a Race Relations Board to investigate allegations of racial discrimination and a Community Relations Commission to promote understanding and tolerance between the different ethnic groups.

Roy Jenkins and multi-culturalism

Roy Jenkins, Home Secretary from 1964 to 1967, was an advocate of multi-culturalism. By this he meant that diverse cultures should be celebrated and equality of opportunity should be open to all irrespective of background. This view found favour with many liberals but was felt by others to exacerbate the white backlash as some felt threatened by those they perceived as foreigners within their midst.

Comparing two sources

Read the two sources below. Your task is to compare content, provenance and tone.

Source	Content
A	
B	
Main similarities and differences	

Source	Provenance
A	
B	
Main similarities and differences	

Source	Language, tone, emphasis
A	
B	
Main similarities and differences	

SOURCE A

From the 'Rivers of Blood' speech by Enoch Powell, given at the Midland Hotel, Birmingham 20 April 1968

A week or two ago I fell into conversation with a constituent, a middle-aged, quite ordinary working man employed in one of our nationalised industries.

After a sentence or two about the weather, he suddenly said: 'If I had the money to go, I wouldn't stay in this country.' I made some deprecatory reply to the effect that even this government wouldn't last for ever; but he took no notice, and continued: 'I have three children, all of them been through grammar school and two of them married now, with family. I shan't be satisfied till I have seen them all settled overseas. In this country in 15 or 20 years' time the black man will have the whip hand over the white man.'

I can already hear the chorus of execration. How dare I say such a horrible thing? How dare I stir up trouble and inflame feelings by repeating such a conversation?

The answer is that I do not have the right not to do so. Here is a decent, ordinary fellow Englishman, who in broad daylight in my own town says to me, his Member of Parliament, that his country will not be worth living in for his children.

In 15 or 20 years, on present trends, there will be in this country three and a half million Commonwealth immigrants and their descendants.

SOURCE B

From a speech by Home Secretary James Callaghan in the House of Commons on 27 February 1968 to introduce the Commonwealth Immigration Act

This Bill, however some may regard it, must be considered at the same time, and in accordance with, the proposal of the Government to introduce a Race Relations Bill which will establish in this country equality of treatment in the very sensitive areas of housing and of jobs, which is to be introduced by the Government during the next six weeks – certainly before Easter. Both these Bills are, in my view and my judgement, essentially parts of a fair and balanced policy on this matter of race relations. I do not discern much tendency to call names. As I have said, everyone is concerned about this issue, and it was no easy decision to introduce a Bill of this sort.

Foreign policy: Vietnam, Europe and decolonisation

Harold Wilson's foreign policy was dominated by relations with the USA and the fear of being overstretched in terms of overseas commitments.

USA and Vietnam

While neither Wilson nor his foreign ministers enjoyed the close relations with the USA of their predecessors, Britain remained a key ally. The USA sought in particular to gain active British support for its involvement in **Vietnam** so it could give the impression of an international campaign rather than one powerful country at war with a smaller one. President Johnson even said a band of pipers would suffice. However, Wilson had no intention of embroiling British troops in what he saw as an unwinnable war although he gave his US allies moral support. This was enough for left-wing critics to accuse the Government of supporting the USA in a brutal conflict.

Anti-Vietnam War protests

Protests culminated in a violent protest outside the US Embassy in Grosvenor Square, London, in April 1968 – but UK protests were nowhere near as significant or sustained as those in other European countries such as France or the FRG (Federal Republic of Germany) or indeed in the USA itself.

Decolonisation including East of Suez

Britain recognised it had overcommitted in terms of foreign commitments, and in 1967 Defence Secretary Denis Healey announced the withdrawal of British forces from bases east of the Suez Canal – including those in Singapore, Malaya and the Persian Gulf. This led to protests from:

● the governments of countries concerned who had relied on Britain for their defence
● the USA who feared it would weaken the defence against Communism.

Nevertheless, it was a case of the Government facing reality: Britain could no longer afford the cost of this commitment, especially as it was committed to nuclear defence and Cold War commitments, for example, in the FRG.

● Decolonisation meant the bases were no longer necessary to Britain's strategic interests.
● Suez had showed British limitations on the world stage.

Having said this, the British had fought some bloody campaigns, for example, in Aden in the modern state of Yemen before withdrawing in 1968.

Rhodesia

Rhodesia remained an unresolved problem throughout the period. White supremacist Prime Minister Iain Smith had declared **UDI** in November 1965. Wilson met Smith twice, in 1966 and 1968, but no agreement was reached – indeed just for talking to Smith Wilson received howls of criticism from black African leaders and left-wing groups at home. Britain imposed economic sanctions but with the support of South Africa and the Portuguese colony of Mozambique the country endured, despite the beginnings of bloody insurrection among the black majority.

Europe

Britain sought closer ties with Europe particularly because of its greater growth rates and indeed reapplied to join the EEC in 1965. President de Gaulle however vetoed membership for the same reasons as in 1961. He did not feel Britain was sufficiently committed to Europe.

RAG – Rate the timeline

Below are an AS-level essay question and a timeline. Read the question, study the timeline and, using three coloured pens, put a red, amber or green star next to the events to show:

- red – events and policies that have no relevance to the question
- amber – events and policies that have some relevance to the question
- green – events and policies that have direct relevance to the question.

'Britain's foreign policy in the 1960s was based on cutting back commitments.' Explain why you agree or disagree with this view.

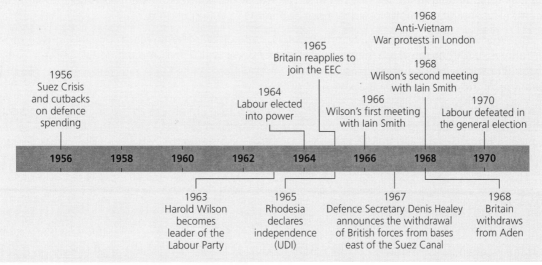

 ## Eliminate irrelevance

Below are a sample A-level essay question and a paragraph written in answer to it. Read the paragraph and identify the parts of the paragraph that are not directly relevant to the question. Draw a line through the information that is irrelevant and justify your deletions in the margin.

'British foreign policy in the 1960s was mainly dictated by the need for reducing its overseas commitments.' Assess the validity of this view.

Britain was forced to reduce its overseas commitments in large part because of the cost. In 1967 Defence Secretary Denis Healey made dramatic cutbacks in Britain's overseas commitments east of the Suez Canal, including those in Singapore and Malaya. Britain had successfully fought a war against communists in Malaya during the 1950s, and the USA had studied these tactics in combatting the Vietcong in Vietnam. This wasn't a question of decolonisation: many leaders opposed these cutbacks because they relied on Britain for defence. Nevertheless Britain could no longer afford these commitments, especially as it was still committed to an independent nuclear deterrent and had its obligations to NATO, for example, in helping defend the FRG through the maintenance of a large garrison there.

However, foreign policy wasn't simply a matter of defending allies. Britain also faced an ongoing problem over the declaration of UDI by Rhodesia in opposition to black majority rule. Prime Minister Harold Wilson met his Rhodesian counterpart Iain Smith on two separate occasions to no avail. Smith enjoyed the support of South Africa and Portuguese colonies such as Mozambique to minimise the impact of economic sanctions, and couldn't predict that he would lose this support as Mozambique gained its own independence in 1974. Wilson moreover was under constant pressure from President Johnson to offer support in the Vietnam War. While Wilson supported the US position in Vietnam, he skilfully avoided British involvement not simply because of the cost — which would have been huge and incongruous with cutbacks elsewhere — but because of the opposition it would generate both from within Britain and elsewhere.

Exam focus

On pages 39–40 is a sample answer to an AS-level question on source evaluation. Read the answer and the comments around it.

SOURCE A

The Albemarle Report (1960) was an investigation into youth work in Britain. It was set up in response to concerns about youth behaviour. It was felt that youth work was in crisis, and much of what was currently offered was unappealing to modern teenagers. The Report advocated considerably more funding and the development of activities which would be more appealing to young people

There are many who leave school lonely or estranged, without ever having learnt to live in the company of their fellows; if they do not learn in adolescence, they never will. The coming together of the young with understanding and helpful adults presents opportunities which can be used in different ways, depending on the traditions of the different organisations and clubs …

Some are too wary or too deeply estranged to accept, at any rate initially, even the slight commitment required by club membership. We should like to see more experiments made to cater for their social needs in the unconstrained way which they appear to seek. We have in mind the coffee bar sited strategically at the sort of place where they tend to congregate …

SOURCE B

From the National Association of Youth Clubs report into events at Brighton on August Bank Holiday 1965

Some of the weekend was perfectly normal, a family seaside holiday situation, but after dark on Saturday and for the 24 hours from Sunday lunchtime, the town had special problems to deal with – problems created by teenage visitors.

Sleeping Rough

Our observers saw the arrival of scores of young teenage boys and girls who had planned to sleep rough. They were moved on by the police and slept on the roofs of public toilets or in fairground huts …

Out for a fight

There was also a minority of youngsters who came looking for trouble. The observers report that Brighton is a Mod town. Forays of rockers turned up throughout the two days and this caused running fights. There were several ugly scenes, including hooliganism in the main shopping street …

Not all of the people involved in fights were young workers … a group of University students … were involved in one 'punch up' … Our young reporter said, 'They had heard there was going to be some trouble and they thought they would come for the sheer hell of it.'

To sum up, most of the boys and girls on the loose in Brighton were looking for excitement; 'kicks' and adventure not for violence. Most of this could constitute nothing more than high spirits but their wandering abroad throughout the night must give cause for concern. Some teenage girls were taken into custody by the police. A few were looking for the chance of a riot …

H Haywood Education Officer

With reference to Sources A and B and your understanding of the historical context, which of these two sources is more valuable in explaining why there were concerns about young people's behaviour in the early 1960s?

Both Sources A and B offer useful insight into why there was concern about young people's behaviour. While Source A emphasises the lack of opportunities for young people and their own lack of social skills, Source B is possibly more critical in suggesting many went to Brighton to look for trouble, in the case of the university students because they were bored, turning up just for the sheer hell of it. There had been concerns about young people since the previous decade, when Teddy Boys were accused of vandalism and violence. It was all a reaction to the post-war baby boom, when the birth-rate increased significantly and, as young people grew up, full employment meant they had disposable income which fuelled interests and indeed lifestyles different from their parents. Both highlight in different ways the dangers originating from the lack of supervision.

Sources addressed in terms of utility from the outset.

Valid context.

However, while both sources express concerns, the fact that Source B is based on investigations by young people themselves suggests their findings may not be typical – in other words they are not writing about all young people. Indeed, even among those who went to Brighton, the actual troublemakers were in a minority. They appear more concerned with the lack of suitable accommodation, noting that many slept on toilet roofs or fairground huts. Similarly the Albemarle Report is concerned with the lack of facilities. Here its provenance may lead to some questions of reliability. It was concerned with the lack of facilities for young people and advocated the provision of more – so it would inevitably emphasise the former to propose the need for the latter. More worrying, possibly, is the inference that young people are lacking social skills and may be alienated. The suggestion is that facilities would have an educational purpose – to have 'helpful adults' who might improve young people's social skills and in so doing improve their confidence.

Limitations to utility.

Relevant content.

Consideration of provenance in terms of utility.

Both sources contain some suggestion of hidden meaning – a desire for control that young people may reject, however well intentioned. Source A suggests young people suffer from loneliness and estrangement which would preclude youth club membership – unless it is made more accessible through a format that young people would like, for example, a coffee bar. This suggests the authorities are attempting to move towards young people's interests. Source B similarly is concerned with lack of supervision or control. It suggests the lack of suitable accommodation at night was a greater concern than the violence – and particularly so for girls, some of whom were arrested presumably to keep them safe.

Sources are compared in terms of content. This is unnecessary, but adds to the quality of the answer.

While both sources are useful, Source B may be more so. It is based on evidence from young researchers and offers concrete examples in support. It suggests, for example, that there are dangers in sleeping rough, that there was more concern for girls than boys in this position, that the troublemakers were untypical – indeed not simply working class either as it highlights the university students who turned up looking for trouble. It is interesting too that Source B offers the voice of one researcher. Source A is written in formal language representative of an official report, for example the use of technical terms such as 'adolescence' and 'estranged' in the first few sentences. Source B on the other hand uses more everyday language including that of young people at the time – 'punch ups', 'kicks'. This ironically makes it read as more authoritative than Source A, the official report.

In conclusion, therefore, while both are useful in highlighting concerns about young people, to show why older people were concerned, Source B offers a more genuine voice because it offers evidence in support and deploys more of the everyday language that young people would recognise. Indeed it is based on research from young people themselves. Source A also highlights valid concerns but is in a more formal language without evidence in support, and indeed could possibly be taking a more patronising view in that it wants facilities to have an educational function of raising young people's social skills. It is also advocating a case and therefore may be less impartial than Source B.

Judgement based on evidence from the source.

Comparison is unnecessary in terms of what is required but still valid.

Conclusion makes a valid judgement and summarises what has been said.

This is an excellent response in terms of utility, addressing content, context, tone and language to arrive at a judgement. It also grounds the sources in relevant background. The comparisons are unnecessary, but they do add to the quality of the answer. This a high Level 5 response.

Find the evidence

The most important element in producing an argument is supporting evidence and examples. Read the essay again and identify where evidence has been used effectively to support an argument.

Exam focus

Below is a sample Level 5 answer to an A-level question on source evaluation. Read the answer and the comments around it.

With reference to Sources A, B (see page 36) and C (see below) and your understanding of the historical context, assess the value of these sources to a historian studying concerns as to the behaviour of young people during the early 1960s.

SOURCE C

From 'Beatles on the Beat', an article which appeared in *The Times* newspaper, 11 November 1963; *The Times* is a well-respected newspaper read mainly by members of the British professional classes

To evade crowds of followers besieging Birmingham Hippodrome tonight, the Beatles were driven to the theatre in a police van and they wore Mackintoshes and helmets.

Some of the crowd, mainly girls in their teens, had waited for ten hours, part of the time in heavy rain. The car in which the singing group travelled from London broke down on the M1 and they were over an hour late in arriving at the Birmingham police headquarters. There, after having tea with the police officers, they borrowed helmets and Mackintoshes and drove to the theatre in the van preceded by decoy police cars. Before the crowd realised it the gates of a yard near the stage door were opened, the car drove in and the gates were closed.

Each of the sources offers insight into why there was concern about young people's behaviour during the early 1960s. Source A emphasises the lack of opportunities for young people and their own lack of social skills. Source B is possibly more critical in suggesting many went to Brighton to look for trouble, in the case of the university students because they were bored, turning up just for the sheer hell of it. Source C meanwhile highlights the efforts necessary to police a Beatles concert at Birmingham Hippodrome and may imply the need for this subterfuge is to prevent disorder, but only weakly so.

> Introduction comments on the content of each source in terms of utility.

Sources A and B highlight in different ways the dangers originating from the lack of supervision while Source C suggests a Beatles concert involves considerable police resources, and fans were committed enough to wait in adverse weather conditions for up to ten hours. All suggest something of an alternative lifestyle and interests among young people as compared to adults, which offered cause for concern.

> It is unnecessary to consider the sources together but can add to quality of answer – here more on historical context could be offered.

However, while all the sources express these concerns, the fact that Source B is based on investigations by young people themselves suggests their findings may not be typical – in other words they are not writing about all young people. Indeed, the authors recognise that even among those who went to Brighton, the actual troublemakers were in a minority. They appear more concerned with the lack of suitable accommodation, noting that many slept on toilet roofs or fairground huts, suggesting a moral disapprobation. This is instructive in offering a comment on attitudes of the time – suggesting that young people are at risk if not supervised and in proper accommodation at night. The Albemarle Report is also concerned with the lack of facilities. Here its provenance may lead to some questions of reliability. It was concerned with the lack of facilities for young people and advocated the provision of more – so it would inevitably emphasise the former to propose the need for the latter. More worrying, possibly, is the inference that young people are lacking social skills and may be alienated. The suggestion is that facilities would have an educational purpose – to have 'helpful adults' who might

> Useful inference from tenor of the source.

> Useful comment on provenance in terms of purpose.

improve young people's social skills and in so doing improve their confidence. Source C, from an establishment newspaper, a broadsheet, almost has a tone of bemusement using words like 'besieging' and emphasising the disguise of helmets and mackintoshes. The inference is that readers would be surprised at this sort of behaviour.

Provenance in terms of language.

All the sources indeed contain some suggestion of hidden meaning – in the case of Sources A and B a desire for control that young people may reject, however well intentioned, and in Source C the cost of deployment of resources for policing the concert that could possibly by implication more valuably be used elsewhere such as decoy police cars. Source A suggests young people suffer from loneliness and estrangement which would preclude youth club membership – unless it is made more accessible through a format that young people would like, for example, a coffee bar. This suggests the authorities are attempting to move towards young people's interests. Source B similarly is concerned with lack of supervision or control. It suggests the lack of suitable accommodation at night was a greater concern than the violence – and particularly so for girls, some of whom were arrested presumably to keep them safe. *The Times* also emphasises that most of the young fans waiting for a long period in the rain are girls.

While all the sources are useful, Source B may be more so. It is based on evidence from young researchers and offers concrete examples in support. It suggests, for example, that there are dangers in sleeping rough, that there was more concern for girls than boys in this position, that the troublemakers were untypical – indeed not simply working class either as it highlights the university students who turned up looking for trouble. It is interesting too that Source B offers the voice of one researcher. Source A is written in formal language representative of an official report, for example, the use of technical terms such as 'adolescence' and 'estranged' in the first few sentences. Source B on the other hand uses more everyday language including that of young people at the time – 'punch ups', 'kicks'. This ironically makes it read as more authoritative than Source A, the official report. Source C reports on the police actions, but doesn't relate enough about adverse behaviour among the crowd or the reasons for the subterfuge. It is rather superficial, telling a story but short on meaning.

Judgement based on evidence from the source.

Valid criticism of Source C.

In conclusion, therefore, while all the sources are useful in highlighting concerns about young people, Source B offers a more genuine voice because it offers evidence in support and deploys more of the everyday language that young people would recognise. Indeed it is based on research from young people themselves. Source A also highlights valid concerns but is in a more formal language without evidence in support, and indeed could possibly be taking a more patronising view in that it wants facilities to have an educational function of raising young people's social skills. It is also advocating a case, therefore may be less impartial than Source B. Source C meanwhile lacks detail and interpretation – most of its import is left to the reader to infer.

Conclusion summarises and makes valid judgement.

This answer shows very good understanding of all three sources in relation to content and provenance and presents a valid argument. There could be more on historical context – indeed more use could have been made of the background information on Source A. However, what historical context is offered is valid in terms of the comments on source utility and the overall judgement, so this would be worthy of a low Level 5.

Find the evidence

The most important element in producing an argument is supporting evidence and examples. Read the essay again and identify where evidence has been used effectively to support an argument.

3 The end of the post-war consensus 1970–79

Heath's government 1970–74

Conservative Edward Heath as conservative leader

Like Wilson, Edward Heath came from a lower middle class background and excelled at Oxford. He reformed the party, reducing the influence of its traditional aristocratic leadership and promoting colleagues on merit – for example, Anthony Barber, who became his Chancellor, and Margaret Thatcher as Education Secretary.

> ### The New Right
>
> Heath was influenced by the thinking of the **New Right** and committed to less government intervention, allowing market forces to decide wages and prices. These ideas were adopted at a conference at Selsdon Park in January 1970 – hence the notion of 'Selsdon Man', a new type of Conservative voter who wanted more control over his own affairs. This reduction in the role of government saw an important break with the post-war consensus.

Economic problems and the impact of the 1973 oil crisis

The Government quickly abandoned its commitment to less intervention by intervening to help key industries in trouble.

- Rolls-Royce, the main producer of aircraft engines, was nationalised in 1971.
- Upper Clyde shipbuilders received a subsidy of £35 million to stay afloat.

1973 oil crisis

Post-war prosperity was largely dependent on cheap fuel. The biggest provider of this was OPEC (Organisation of Petroleum Exporting Countries), based mainly in the Middle East. In September 1973, a major war broke out between Israel and its Arab neighbours. OPEC both reduced its supply of oil and raised prices as a response to perceived Western support for Israel – from US $2 to US $35 a barrel between 1973 and 1980. The age of cheap fuel was over.

Effects of the oil crisis

- There were severe shortages of fuel for industry and petrol for transport.
- Imports became more expensive, and the value of sterling was further reduced. The value of the £1 fell to US $1.50. This led to huge budget deficits.
- After having fallen slightly in the early 1970s, inflation grew again – to 16 per cent by 1974.
- Unemployment doubled – from 785,000 in 1973 to 1,608,000 by 1978.

In February, Heath called an election on the basis of 'Who governs Britain?' The overall result was tight: no party had an overall majority and Labour would only be able to govern with the help of the Liberals.

Northern Ireland

In August 1971 the Government introduced **internment** to try to remove potential troublemakers by arresting them without trial. Internment netted mainly innocent people.

The problems were compounded in January 1972 with 'Bloody Sunday' where British troops opened fire on Catholic protesters in Londonderry. Fourteen were killed. The IRA retaliated with the beginning of a bombing campaign on mainland Britain.

Direct rule and the Sunningdale Agreement

Britain meanwhile suspended the Stormont parliament and adopted **direct rule** from Westminster. Most politicians agreed some degree of power sharing between Catholics and Protestants was necessary. In December 1973 the Secretary of State for Northern Ireland, Willie Whitelaw, introduced the Sunningdale Agreement, which attempted this through the formation of a new executive made up of representatives from both communities which would govern the province. However, **hard-line Protestants** influenced in particular by the Reverend Ian Paisley paralysed the province by a fifteen-day strike which defeated the agreement.

Identify the tone and emphasis of a source a

Study Source A below. Don't focus on the content, instead concentrate and write notes on:

- the language
- the sentence structure
- the emphasis of the source
- the overall tone.

SOURCE A

From Anthony Bailey, 'On the Oldpark, Belfast', the *New Yorker* 1973; Anthony Bailey was an American journalist who covered the Troubles mainly for the *New Yorker* magazine

The gulf is deep, and has some obvious causes. The Catholics for a long time were gerrymandered out of adequate political representation. They have borne the brunt of unemployment. And the Protestants, because they know the Catholics have indeed good reason for deep dissatisfaction with the state of Ulster, are terrified of Catholic cohesion –the unity established among the Catholics by their church, their schools and the great injustice done to them … This gulf has in other ways been deepened and exploited by generations of Ulster politicians, who have found great personal benefit in maintaining what, to all intents and purposes, has been an intermittent working class civil war. They have encouraged the belief of Catholics and Protestants that they are fundamentally different from one another.

Identify the significance of provenance a

Look at what is said about Source B.

- Who said it?
- What type of source it is?
- When it was said?
- Where it was said?
- Crucially, what was the speaker's purpose?

What does this suggest about its value as a source of evidence about the Troubles in Northern Ireland?

SOURCE B

From an Ulster Defence Association leaflet that appeared in Protestant areas of Northern Ireland in 1971; the UDA was a Protestant political and paramilitary group associated primarily with the defence of Protestant areas in Ulster

Being convinced that the enemies of Faith and Freedom are determined to destroy the state of Northern Ireland and thereby enslave the people of God, we call on all members of our loyalist institutions, and other responsible citizens, to organise themselves immediately into platoons of twenty under the command of someone capable of acting as sergeant. Every effort must be made to arm these platoons with whatever weapons are available … the first duty of each platoon will be to formulate a plan for the defence of its own street or road in cooperation with platoons in adjoining areas. A structure of command is already in existence and the various platoons will eventually be linked in a coordinated effort.

Industrial relations and the miners' strikes

Industrial relations

Edward Heath came to power determined to reform industrial relations, to enjoy success where Labour had failed with its White Paper 'In Place of Strife'. One problem was that many strikes were unofficial. Power lay with local shop stewards rather than the official union leadership, and industrial action could be called by a show of hands. In this respect it was difficult to control. To address the issue Heath's government passed the 1971 Industrial Relations Act.

1971 Industrial Relations Act

This was designed to be a strong response to the growing problem of industrial action but it was deeply resented by the union movement.
● A National Industrial Relations Court was set up to judge the validity of any strike.
● Unions had to register and could face fines if any industrial action was felt to be unwarranted.

The trade unions, however, refused to co-operate. They refused to register or acknowledge the Industrial Relations Court. The 1971 Industrial Relations Act was a failure and was dropped.

This led to something of a free-for-all in terms of industrial relations, with the number of strikes growing from 228 in 1971 to 2,873 by 1973 – but proportionally with far more days lost, emphasising their severity.

The National Union of Miners and the miners' strikes

The **National Union of Miners (NUM)** appeared to lead the way in threatening the Government. It faced significant pit closures through unprofitability and felt it was fighting for the livelihood of its members. A strike against closures and for more pay in 1972 involved successful tactics such as the use of **flying pickets** and mass rallies to blockade coal distribution centres to prevent its movement. In 1973 the miners won their battle – and a 21 per cent pay increase – and returned the following year with a further pay demand.

This coincided with the 1973 oil crisis.

The three-day week

The oil crisis coincided with the rejection of a 13 per cent pay offer by the miners and a ballot on a national strike. In the face of fuel shortages, Heath responded with the imposition of a three-day working week. There was a sense of crisis with shortened TV hours, power cuts and encouragement for people to share baths.

The three-day week suggested Britain was in deep trouble although some have suggested the concentration of production into three days actually in some cases saw it increase. Nevertheless there was a sense that Britain could run out of fuel and its economy would be seriously weakened. Heath called for a general election on the question of 'Who governs Britain?' This was set for February 1974.

The February 1974 election

The Conservatives would in fact be judged not on their battle with the miners but on their economic record. Both inflation and unemployment were rising and of course industrial action was not just confined to the NUM. It was a tight result, with Labour only able to take power with the support of the fourteen Liberal MPs. The new Government found it inherited the same problems.

RAG – Rate the factors

Read the A-level question below and the factors listed to answer it. Using three coloured pens, put a red, amber or green star next to the factors to show:

- red – factors that have no relevance to the question
- amber – factors that have some relevance to the question
- green – factors that are directly relevant to the question.

'The Conservatives lost the February 1974 election largely as a result of the three-day week.' Assess the validity of this statement.

- Selsdon Man
- The thinking of the New Right
- The failure of the 1971 Industrial Relations Act
- The miners' industrial action 1972–73
- The growth in unofficial strikes called by local shop stewards
- The imposition of a three-day week
- The situation in Northern Ireland
- The 1973 oil crisis
- Economic problems such as growing inflation and unemployment.

Now repeat the activity with the following A-level question:

'Continued industrial action caused the defeat of the Conservatives in the February 1974 election.' Assess the validity of this statement.

Eliminate irrelevance

Below is a sample paragraph in response to the second question above. Read the paragraph and identify the parts of the paragraph that are not directly relevant to the question. Draw a line through the information that is irrelevant and justify your deletions in the margin.

The Conservative government faced continued industrial action between 1970 and 1974. It also faced problems such as inflation, unemployment and the 1973 oil crisis which ended the era of cheap fuel. Britain's economy had been dependent on cheap fuel. The oil crisis was a result of Arab suppliers cutting off supplies because they believed western countries were too friendly with Israel. However, industrial unrest was difficult to contain as much was unofficial, called by local shop stewards by a show of hands, often without even consulting union leaders. The government's response, the 1971 Industrial Relations Act, had failed because unions failed either to register or acknowledge the authority of the National Industrial Relations Court. In a sense this non-co-operation of unions was to dog the four years of Conservative government and from the outset was a contributory factor to its defeat in February 1974.

The Labour governments of Wilson and Callaghan 1974-79

REVISED

Labour governments 1974-79

Political, economic and industrial problems

The economic crises, particularly in terms of inflation, which had faced Heath, worsened under Labour.

- Commodity prices had increased 160 per cent between 1971 and 1974.
- The ending of fixed exchange rates in 1972 allowed money to find its own value in open markets: sterling fell in value, making imports more expensive and inflation difficult to control.
- When Britain joined the EEC in 1973 it had to phase out preferable tariffs with Commonwealth countries and introduce the **Common Agricultural Policy (CAP)**. Food prices rose.

The Government's principal policy to combat inflation was the **Social Contract**. The Government repealed the 1971 Industrial Relations Act, ended statutory wage and price controls and expanded welfare provision and nationalisation in return for wage restraint in pay claims. Chancellor of the Exchequer Denis Healey's first budget, for example, saw increases in pension benefits and food and housing subsidies to help the poorest groups in society while higher taxes and cuts in the defence budget helped finance these. However, economic problems mounted.

- The budget deficit grew.
- The National Enterprise Board was set up in 1975 officially to invest in any firms, not just ailing ones. However, in practice it concentrated on those in trouble to save jobs:
  - In 1975 it invested heavily in **British Leyland**.
  - In 1976 shipbuilding and British Aerospace were nationalised.

Although the number of strikes fell, inflation grew – from 16 per cent in 1974 to 24 per cent in 1975. The TUC accepted maximum pay rises of £6 per week. This helped reduce inflation to 16.5 per cent in 1976.

IMF loan

In 1976, with the deficit continuing, the exchange rate collapsed from £1 to US $2.75 in 1975 to US $1.70 by May 1976 and US $1.50 by October. In November, the Government had to apply to the **International Monetary Fund (IMF)** for a loan of £3 billion. The condition was deflationary measures including reductions in government spending – 7 per cent in 1978 while sterling gradually increased in value and revenues from North Sea oil and gas began to appear.

Industrial relations problems

However, more and greater problems lay ahead. Union leader Jack Jones retired and his successor Moss Evans was less supportive of the Social Contract. Ford workers were granted a pay rise of 17 per cent in autumn 1978. Lorry drivers struck for significant pay increases, bringing the transport network to a halt before accepting increases of 20 per cent – and then low-paid public sector workers went on strike. The scene was set for the **winter of discontent**, which saw dustbins unemptied, hospital workers on strike and, in extreme circumstances, Liverpool cemetery workers refusing to bury the dead.

Labour's special relationship with the unions had clearly broken down. Callaghan had delayed calling an election in autumn 1978, not having foreseen the crisis, so it was unsurprising that when he did the Conservatives won with an overall majority of 70. Thatcher's government would be very different.

Northern Ireland

The Troubles continued in Northern Ireland, and the IRA continued their bombing and terror campaign both in Britain and by targeting British soldiers serving in mainland Europe. In August 1979 they assassinated Lord Mountbatten, who was related by marriage to the royal family and a famous Establishment figure; and eighteen British soldiers were killed in one ambush at Warrenpoint.

Simple essay style

Below is a sample A-level exam-style question. Use your own knowledge and the information on the opposite page to produce a plan for this question. Choose four general points and provide three pieces of specific evidence to support each general point.

Once you have planned your essay, write the introduction and conclusion for the essay.

The introduction should list the points discussed in the essay.

The conclusion should summarise the key points and justify which point was the most important.

'The Labour government 1974 to 1979 was dominated by economic difficulties.' How far do you agree with this statement?

RAG – Rate the factors

Read the A-level question below and the factors listed to answer it. Using three coloured pens, put a red, amber or green star next to the factors to show:

- red – factors that have no relevance to the question
- amber – factors that have some significance to the question
- green – factors that are directly relevant to the question.

How far do you agree that Labour lost the 1979 election because of its mishandling of industrial relations?

- Labour repealed the 1971 Industrial Relations Act
- Labour won two elections in 1974 with a narrow majority
- The coal miners had won significant wage increases through bouts of industrial action between 1972 and 1974
- Heath had imposed a three-day week on industry
- Commodity prices rose 160 per cent between 1971 and 1974
- Food prices rose after Britain had joined the EEC in 1973
- The Common Agricultural Policy guaranteed farmers the EEC would buy up their surpluses
- The Social Contract ended statutory wage and price controls
- The National Enterprise Board was set up in 1975
- Britain had to apply for an IMF loan in 1976
- Ford and transport workers won significant wage increases in 1978
- The winter of discontent saw industrial action by low-paid public sector workers
- The winter of discontent symbolised the end of the Social Contract.

Now apply this activity to the following question:

'Industrial unrest was the biggest economic and social problem faced by the Labour governments from 1974 to 1979.' How far do you agree with this statement?

The reasons for Labour's defeat in 1979

Many commentators expected James Callaghan to hold an election in autumn 1978. The economy appeared to be recovering, although inflation and unemployment remained high and he enjoyed personal popularity. However, he decided to wait until 1979 when, it was hoped, there would be even more significant economic improvement. This was a fateful decision that led some critics to suggest that the Conservatives did not win the subsequent election so much as Labour lost it.

Problems for the Labour government

The government faced considerable problems that worsened in the latter months of 1978 and culminated in the winter of discontent (see page 48).

- Callaghan had hoped to extend the Social Contract. However, with unemployment at 1.4 million, inflation at over 10 per cent and suggested pay increases to be limited to 5 per cent, this was unlikely. Indeed not only the TUC but the Labour Party itself rejected any renewal at its autumn 1978 conference.
- This rejection led to a spate of strikes including those of low-paid public sector workers whose wage increases had been squeezed during the three-year period of the Social Contract.
- Labour's biggest support base, the manufacturing industry, was in decline. Manufacturing itself fell from 34 to 30 per cent of national output during the years 1970 to 1977 when as many as 2 million jobs may have been lost.
- Politically, Labour had been dependent on support from the Liberals. However, the formal Lib–Lab Pact signed in 1977 was not renewed. This left Labour relying on the support of Scottish Nationalist Party MPs. The price for this had been some measure of devolution. However, when this failed in a **referendum** the SNP withdrew its support, leaving Labour a minority government.

Sensing victory, the Conservatives called a vote of no confidence in the Government on 28 March 1979. The Government lost the motion by one vote – but it was close enough for the Government to resign and call an election.

Why the Conservatives won

While Labour appeared tired, the Conservatives were buoyant. Margaret Thatcher had proved an effective leader since ousting Edward Heath in 1975. The party contracted the firm Saatchi & Saatchi to organise a modern advertising campaign, one of whose centrepieces was giant posters on unemployment with the slogan, 'Labour isn't working'.

Conservative manifesto 1979

The Conservative manifesto targeted the middle classes and their fears.

- They offered more spending on police and defence.
- They promised to introduce union reform so the industrial unrest of the previous decade could not be repeated.

However, they also spoke to the aspirational working classes, who sought to better themselves. Particularly popular was the policy to sell council houses at cost price to tenants.

Where policies were more controversial, such as the economic ideas of the New Right and **monetarism** (see page 64), the manifesto was vague.

The Conservatives' electoral strategies worked. They won a majority of 43 and the scene was set for significant political change.

Comparing two alternative answers

Read the two sources, the question and the extracts from two answers. Compare them in terms of content, provenance and tone. Which answer do you conclude is the more valuable?

With reference to Sources A and B, and your understanding of the historical context, assess the value of these sources to a historian studying the reasons for the Conservative victory in the 1979 General Election.

Answer 1

Source A is from a diary and reflects the dismay of the author in terms of the winter of discontent. There is a cynical tone of frustration with the strikes, the smaller size of newspapers, the discontent people were feeling. However, this is only one person's view. Source B is taken from the Conservative manifesto and to some extent it echoes the frustration, clearly blaming the unions, whom it accuses of extremism and preventing Britain from enjoying economic success. Its tone suggests disappointment at the situation – Britain is held to ransom by unions whom it accuses of abusing liberties ...

Answer 2

Source A is from a diary in which the author is clearly fed up with union activity. He's not alone; he mentions other people at the bookstall feeling the same way. This is useful in that it shows the frustrations that would lead many people to vote Conservative. Source B is taken from the Conservative manifesto and is very useful because it also blames the unions, suggesting they're extremists and they're feared.

SOURCE A

Extracts from *The Kenneth Williams Diaries*; Kenneth Williams was a much-loved comic actor and raconteur with markedly right-wing views

Thursday 4 January 1979

Up at 7.30 to get the papers: all the talk at the bookstall was about the utter hatred of unions and strikes etc.: one day I think this loathing will be channelled into action ...

Wednesday 10 January

Saw the news: Callaghan arrived back from Guadeloupe saying 'There is no chaos', which is a euphemistic way of talking about the lorry drivers ruining all production and work in the entire country, but one admires his phlegm ...

Monday 5 February

The TV news was about strikes galore and the mounting refuse has caused the authorities to set rat bait down and spray the stuff with disinfectant!

SOURCE B

Conservative Party manifesto 1979

THIS ELECTION is about the future of Britain – a great country which seems to have lost its way.

During the industrial strife of last winter, confidence, self-respect, common sense, and even our sense of common humanity were shaken. At times this society seemed on the brink of disintegration ...

[B]y heaping privilege without responsibility on the trade unions, Labour have given a minority of extremists the power to abuse individual liberties and to thwart Britain's chances of success. One result is that the trade union movement, ... is today more distrusted and feared than ever before.

Society in the 1970s

Society in the 1970s continued to reflect the growing assertiveness of women, youth conflict and racial tensions.

Women

Two important pieces of legislation were the Equal Pay Act of 1970 and Sex Discrimination Act of 1975.

The Equal Pay Act 1970

After years of struggles (see pages 14 and 32) the Equal Pay Act was finally passed in 1970 to come into effect by 1975. One reason for its passage was that it was a pre-condition of joining the EEC.

Sex Discrimination Act 1975

This set up the Equal Opportunities Commission to ensure that fair employment practices were observed and that women had legal protection against discrimination in education and employment. It established tribunals to deal with workplace and everyday sexual harassment.

The progress of feminism

Women's groups continued to campaign for wider women's rights such as the ending of domestic violence and the right to birth control and abortion. The early 1970s saw rape crisis centres and refuges for battered wives and their children being opened: Erin Pizzey was influential here, setting up the first women's refuge at Chiswick in London. Many women became activists, for example, protesting against the Miss World Competition in 1970 and setting up the magazine *Spare Rib* which linked women's subjugation to class oppression.

Youth

The 1970s saw the continuation of football hooliganism, in which areas around football grounds could, on match days, become no-go areas for non-football fans. The later years saw the beginnings of punk rock, loud angry music followed by fans who seemed to challenge traditional values by their appearance of torn clothing, body piercing, chains and spiked hair. However, as with other trends, this was for most simply a rebellious phase.

Race and immigration

This continued to cause tensions, for example, through accusations of racist policing. In particular black youths became angry at the apparently unfair use of **'Stop and Search'** procedures, which were overwhelmingly used against black people. There was some concern that integration hadn't worked and different ethnic communities rarely mixed.

1976 Race Relations Act

This outlawed indirect discrimination – where discrimination was hidden, for example, a job interviewee not being appointed because he was black but not being informed of the reason. It also created a new Commission for Racial Equality to police discrimination.

Black protest

Black people's protests against racism sometimes resulted in violent clashes with police. On one such occasion, in 1979, a white protester, Blair Peach, a teacher from New Zealand, was killed. The police meanwhile tried on several occasions unsuccessfully to prevent the Notting Hill Carnival from taking place due to fears of disorder. In the early 1970s a British version of the Black Panthers, a violent US Black Power movement, appeared. While there was considerable unrest, however, the decade avoided riots on the scale of those in 1960s USA.

White backlash

The 1970s saw the emergence of a new extreme right-wing party, the National Front, which briefly enjoyed electoral success – with its leader Martin Webster polling 16 per cent of the vote in a West Bromwich by-election in May 1973. They held noisy, provocative demonstrations that attracted skinheads and other disaffected young people – but more opposed them in the Anti-Nazi League and the Rock Against Racism movement supported by many popular musicians of the day.

Spectrum of importance

Below are a sample A-level exam-style question and a list of general points that could be used to answer the question. Use your own knowledge and the information on the opposite page to reach a judgement about the importance of these general points to the question posed. Write numbers on the spectrum below to indicate their relative importance. Having done this, write a brief justification of your placement, explaining why some of these factors are more important than others.

How far were tensions in British society in the 1970s driven by racial and gender issues?

1 Violence at football grounds

2 Punk rock

3 Equal Pay and Sex Discrimination Acts

4 Rape Crisis Centres

5 National Front

6 Stop and Search

7 Anti-Nazi League

8 Death of Blair Peach

9 Notting Hill Carnival

←───→

Least important   Most important

Turning assertion into argument

Below are a series of definitions, a sample exam-style question and two sample conclusions. One of the conclusions achieves a high mark because it contains an argument. The other achieves a lower mark because it contains only description and assertion. Identify which is which. The mark scheme on page 7 will help you.

A description is a detailed account; an assertion is a statement of fact or an opinion that is not supported by a reason; a reason is a statement that explains or justifies something; an argument is an assertion justified with a reason.

To what extent were divisions in society in the 1970s a result of racial and generational tensions?

Conclusion 1

Divisions in society resulted largely from racial and generational tensions. There was a lot of racism. Blair Peach was killed on 23 April 1979 during a protest against the National Front in Southall. The protest turned violent and over 40 were injured. However it wasn't just racism that caused tensions – older people were worried about the violence caused by young people. They were concerned too about punk rock which they thought was loud and tuneless. Most young people were neither violent nor punk rockers.

Conclusion 2

While there were undoubtedly generational and racial tensions, most people lived in harmony in the 1970s. There were concerns about violence among young people, especially at football matches, but most supporters avoided fighting. Punk rock may have challenged older people who questioned its values and disliked the appearance of its adherents, but again most young people weren't punk rockers, and even for those that were it was largely a phase they grew out of like the mods and Teddy Boys of earlier decades. While there were undoubtedly racial tensions we should also remember that the National Front never enjoyed widespread support or electoral success and many young people joined organisations such as Rock Against Racism. While there were tensions in the 1970s the coherence of society was never threatened, and one can usually discern similar tensions in earlier periods.

Foreign policy: entry in the EEC and attitudes during developments in the Cold War

The 1970s saw Britain more involved in Europe than with the superpowers.

Britain's entry into and relations with the EEC

Britain finally joined the EEC in January 1973 together with Eire and Denmark. De Gaulle's successor, Georges Pompidou, was more supportive of British entry and saw Britain as a bulwark against the economic domination of the FRG. Edward Heath himself was pro-Europe and membership seemed a reward for his failed efforts during the 1960s.

Attitudes to membership

The issue of membership split the country, particularly over issues of **sovereignty**. Many were afraid EEC law would supersede national law, while the Labour Party was split over what membership would mean for trade union rights and working conditions. While in opposition the left-wing leader Tony Benn called for a referendum on the issue: he was convinced the majority of the electorate opposed membership.

1975 Referendum

After Labour came to power the promised referendum took place. Most political leaders and influential groups supported membership. In the event, those supporting membership won 67 per cent of the vote – although one-third of the electorate did not vote so the majority was not wholly convincing.

Problems with membership

Britain was rarely an enthusiastic member moreover. Politicians constantly complained that Britain's contribution to the EEC budget was far too high, while the Common Agricultural Policy (CAP) was a particular bone of contention. Here farmers were guaranteed prices for surplus production: the policy favoured inefficient farmers such as many in France while it disadvantaged more efficient farmers such as those in Britain who did not produce surpluses. British fishermen complained also that European fishermen were depleting stocks by extensive fishing techniques.

Special relationship with the USA

While Heath was far more interested in Europe than the USA, Britain maintained its relationship with the USA although it was not so close as in the 1950s and early 1970s.

Relations with USSR and China

Relations with Communist China were particularly fraught during the 1960s. Not only was the anti-western Cultural Revolution in full swing, but Chinese leader Mao Tse Tung saw it as a way to win back Hong Kong, a British colony off the Chinese mainland. Chinese agents fomented terrorism within Hong Kong which saw five policemen killed.

However, in the 1970s relations improved – in part because the USA improved its relations with China. President Nixon attempted to build up a USA–Chinese alliance to worry the Soviet Union. However, Edward Heath also visited China in 1974 and received both a warm welcome and two giant pandas to bring to a British zoo. With the death of Mao in 1976 the regime became far more amenable to Britain, and trade links and cultural ties developed.

Relations with the Soviet Union meanwhile remained frosty. Not only was the Soviet Union concerned about Britain's closer relations with its enemy, China, but Britain was concerned about KGB activity in London – for example, in 1978 when a Bulgarian dissident was murdered in a London street by the tip of an umbrella soaked in poison. There were also rumours that senior Labour and trade union leaders – including, incredibly, Harold Wilson himself – were KGB agents.

Turning assertion to argument

Below are a sample exam-style question and a series of assertions. Read the question and then add a justification to each of the assertions to turn it into an argument.

'Britain's foreign policies in the 1970s were dominated by membership of the European Economic Community.' How far do you agree with this statement?

Membership of the EEC split Britain particularly over issues of sovereignty.

Britain remained an unenthusiastic member of the EEC during the 1970s.

Britain remained a loyal supporter of the USA.

Britain's relationship with the USSR was fraught during the 1970s.

Recommended reading

- George L. Bernstein, *The Myth of Decline*, pages 199–275 (2004)
- Alwyn W. Turner, *Crisis? What Crisis? Britain in the 1970s*, pages 3–59 (2008)
- A.N. Wilson, *Our Times*, pages 205–271 (2008)

Exam focus

Below is a sample Level 5 answer to an AS-level question. Read the answer and the comments around it.

'Industrial relations were at the heart of the problems facing the economy during the period 1970 to 1979.' Explain why you agree or disagree with this statement.

Industrial relations were a difficult issue throughout the 1970s. The Conservative government of Edward Heath came to power determined to see industrial action more closely regulated. Heath's policy was unsuccessful in the face of union opposition and the Labour government of 1974 to 1979 attempted a Social Contract to formulate agreement with unions. This had already broken down before the winter of discontent in 1979. Clearly then industrial relations had an adverse effect on the economy – but they were not the only factor to do so during the 1970s.

Introduction is focused on the question and shows other factors will also be considered to give a balanced view.

The Conservative government elected in 1970 was determined to regulate the ability of unions to undertake industrial action. It passed the 1971 Industrial Relations Act which set up an Industrial Relations Court to judge the validity of any strike and required unions to register to maintain their legal rights. Unfortunately the unions refused to co-operate either by registering or accepting the authority of the court.

Assertion is supported by factual information to offer a valid reason.

Matters came to a head in 1972 when the National Union of Miners undertook industrial action both in respect of a pay claim and in protest at closures of unprofitable pits. Fuel and electricity supplies were disrupted as the NUM undertook tactics using flying pickets to prevent the movement of coal to power stations. The miners won their fight – and were to do so again the following year when they rejected a pay offer of 13 per cent. Here their industrial action coincided with the oil crisis and led to the imposition of a three-day working week.

It seemed that industrial action had dominated Heath's economic policies. The three-day week gave the impression of a national crisis. In 1974, Labour returned to power and gave in to the union demands. Labour, in part financed by unions, was expected to have a close relationship with them. The new Government repealed the 1971 Industrial Relations Act, ended statutory wage and price controls and expanded welfare provision and nationalisation in return for wage restraint in pay claims. This policy was known as the Social Contract and saw the number of strikes fall from 2,922 in 1974 to 2,282 by 1975, with the number of actual days lost falling more significantly from 14,750 to 6,012. The TUC meanwhile accepted maximum pay rises of £6 per week. This helped reduce inflation to 16.5 per cent in 1976.

Factual information is given in support without swamping the point.

However, by that year the Social Contract was becoming less important and a return to free collective bargaining saw significant wage settlements by stronger unions.

This led to a resurgence of industrial unrest, for example, industrial action by Ford workers which gave them a 17 per cent settlement. Lorry drivers struck for significant pay increases, bringing the transport network to a halt before accepting increases of 20 per cent – and then low-paid public sector workers went on strike. The resultant winter of discontent seemed to symbolise all that was wrong with industrial relations as dustbins went unemptied, hospital workers struck and Liverpool cemetery workers refused to bury the dead. Any special relationship between Labour and the unions had clearly broken down.

Introduction of cause and consequence.

While industrial unrest was clearly a significant factor in the economic problems facing Britain in the 1970s, it was not however the only one. The economic crisis in 1973, which indirectly led to the three-day week and the fall of the Conservative government in 1974, was caused by the oil crisis. Post-war prosperity had been largely dependent on cheap fuel. The biggest provider of this was OPEC (Organisation of Petroleum Exporting Countries), based mainly in the Middle East. In September 1973, a major war broke out between Israel and its Arab neighbours. OPEC both reduced its supply of oil and dramatically raised prices from $2 to $35 a barrel as a response to what it considered as Western support for Israel. The ending of the age of cheap fuel had dramatic effects both in the short and long term. In the immediate period, there were severe shortages of fuel for industry and petrol for transport. While supply was later restored at much higher prices, imports also became more expensive, and the value of sterling was further reduced. At home, falling demand led to unemployment doubling – from 785,000 in 1973 to 1,608,000 by 1978 – while inflation rose as the value of the pound fell to £1 to $1.50 by October 1976.

Striking a balance in terms of the question.

The oil crisis added to problems faced by industry. The Labour government set up a National Enterprise Board in 1975 to invest in industrial development. However, in practice it concentrated on those in financial trouble, investing heavily in British Leyland, for example. Despite this British industry was often less competitive than its foreign competitors, partly as a result of industrial action and partly because of less efficient methods of production and management. Britain faced a huge balance of payments deficit in addition to the falling value of sterling. In November 1976, the Government had to apply to the IMF for a loan of £3 billion. The conditions imposed included reductions in government spending – 7 per cent in 1978 while sterling gradually increased in value and revenues from North Sea oil and gas began to appear.

Weaker assertion – this is the first time this factor has been introduced and it isn't well supported or explained.

It can be seen therefore that while industrial relations were a significant factor in economic problems, there were others too. Britain gained a reputation as being strike prone and beset with poor industrial relations. However, British industry was often less competitive because of inefficient methods of production and management. The 1973 oil crisis led to further problems in that the days of cheap fuel on which industry had largely depended were over. The need for the IMF loan saw economic retrenchment, which further depressed industry, although there was the promise of revenues from North Sea oil and gas. Nevertheless the winter of discontent seemed to summarise all that was wrong with industrial relations and indeed its impact on the economy. It was this probably that defeated the Labour government in 1979 and introduced a Conservative government whose attitude to industrial relations and indeed the economy as a whole was going to be very different.

Conclusion offers a balance in terms of the question.

This essay would reach Level 5 because it shows good understanding of the demands of the question – not just about industrial unrest but other factors which led to economic problems. However, it is not perfect – the comments about the failings in industry are not well developed. It does however show conceptual awareness, for example, of cause and consequence.

Exam focus

This essay is successful because it maintains a strong focus on the question throughout. There is a lot of detail on industrial relations in the introduction and conclusion but other paragraphs are also related to industrial relations where possible. Go through the essay and underline every mention of 'industrial relations'. Next look at an essay you have written and underline your use of key words. Can you improve on your own efforts in the light of what you have seen here?

Exam focus

Below is a sample Level 5 answer to an A-level essay question. Read it and the comments around it.

'Industrial relations were at the heart of the problems facing the economy during the period 1970 to 1979.' Assess the validity of this view.

Industrial relations were a difficult issue throughout the 1970s. The Conservative government of Edward Heath came to power determined to build upon the policy unsuccessfully pursued by the previous Labour government as outlined in the White Paper 'In Place of Strife', which would see industrial action more closely regulated. Heath's policy was no more successful in the face of union intransigence, and the ensuing Labour government attempted a Social Contract to formulate agreement with unions. This broke down in the face of the disastrous winter of discontent in 1973. Clearly then industrial relations had an adverse effect on the economy – but they were not the only factor to do so during the 1970s.

The Conservative government elected in 1970 was determined to regulate the growing propensity of unions to undertake industrial action through the 1971 Industrial Relations Act. This set up an Industrial Relations Court to judge the validity of any strike, with the power to impose fines if a strike it considered unwarranted went ahead, and required unions to register to maintain their legal rights. Unfortunately the unions refused to co-operate either by registering or accepting the authority of the Court.

Matters came to a head in 1972 when the National Union of Miners undertook industrial action both in respect of a pay claim and in protest at closures of unprofitable pits. Fuel and electricity supplies were disrupted as the NUM undertook tactics using flying pickets to prevent the movement of coal to power stations. The miners won their fight – and were to do so again the following year when they rejected a pay offer of 13 per cent. Here their industrial action coincided with the oil crisis and led to the imposition of a three-day working week.

It seemed that industrial action had dominated Heath's economic policies. The three-day week curtailed production and gave the impression of crisis. In 1974, Labour returned to power and gave in to the union demands. Labour, in part financed by unions, was expected to have a closer relationship with them than the Conservatives. The new Government repealed the 1971 Industrial Relations Act, ended statutory wage and price controls and expanded welfare provision and nationalisation in return for wage restraint in pay claims. This policy was known as the Social Contract and saw the number of strikes fall from 2,922 in 1974 to 2,282 by 1975, with the number of actual days lost falling more significantly from 14,750 to 6,012. The TUC meanwhile accepted maximum pay rises of £6 per week. This helped reduce inflation to 16.5 per cent in 1976.

However, by that year the Social Contract was becoming less important and a return to free collective bargaining saw significant wage settlements by stronger unions.

This led to a resurgence of industrial unrest, for example, industrial action by Ford workers which gave them a 17 per cent settlement – far in advance of any recommended by the Government. Lorry drivers struck for significant pay increases, bringing the transport network to a halt before accepting increases of 20 per cent – and then low-paid public sector workers went on strike. The resultant winter of discontent seemed to symbolise all that was wrong with industrial relations as dustbins went unemptied, hospital workers struck and Liverpool cemetery workers refused to bury the dead.

Introduction is focused on question and shows other factors will also be considered to give a balanced view.

Assertion supported by factual information to offer a valid reason.

Other factors are introduced to strike a balance but not developed at this point, thereby maintaining industrial relations focus

Factual information usefully displayed in support.

Enough narrative offered to explain point, but does not dominate it.

While industrial unrest was clearly a significant factor in the economic problems facing Britain in the 1970s, it was not however the only one. The catalyst for the economic crisis in 1973, which indirectly led to the three-day week and fall of the Conservative government in 1974, was the oil crisis. Post-war prosperity had been largely dependent on cheap fuel. The biggest provider of this was OPEC (Organisation of Petroleum Exporting Countries), based mainly in the Middle East. In September 1973, a major war broke out between Israel and its Arab neighbours. OPEC both reduced its supply of oil and dramatically raised prices from $2 to $35 a barrel as a response to what it considered as Western support for Israel. The ending of the age of cheap fuel had dramatic effects both in the short and long term. In the immediate period, there were severe shortages of fuel for industry and petrol for transport. While supply was later restored at much higher prices, imports also became more expensive, and the value of sterling was further reduced. At home, falling demand led to unemployment doubling – from 785,000 in 1973 to 1,608,000 by 1978 while inflation rose as the value of the pound fell to £1 to $1.50 by October 1976.

> Beginning to strike a balance in terms of question. Other factors considered

> Division into short- and long-term factors to widen the argument.

The oil crisis added to problems faced by industry. The Labour government set up a National Enterprise Board in 1975 to invest in industrial development. However, in practice it concentrated on those in trouble to save jobs, investing heavily in British Leyland, for example. Despite this, British industry was often less competitive than its foreign competitors, partly as a result of industrial action and partly because of less efficient methods of production and management. Britain faced a huge balance of payments deficit in addition to the falling value of sterling. In November 1976, the Government had to apply to the IMF for a loan of £3 billion. The condition was deflationary measures including reductions in government spending – 7 per cent in 1978 while sterling gradually increased in value and revenues from North Sea oil and gas began to appear.

> Weaker assertion – this is the first time this factor has been introduced and it isn't well supported or explained.

It can be seen therefore that while industrial relations were a significant factor in economic problems, there were others too. Indeed they tended to interact. British industry was often less competitive because of inefficient methods of production and management, which added to industrial relations problems in the sense that the strategies and procedures for constructive dialogue were often inadequate. However, the 1973 oil crisis led to further problems in that the days of cheap fuel on which industry had largely depended were over. This in turn led to greater militancy among the miners, who saw coal becoming increasingly important again in the face of threats from pit closures. The need for the IMF loan saw economic retrenchment, which further depressed industry, although there was the promise of revenues from North Sea oil and gas. Nevertheless the winter of discontent seemed to summarise all that was wrong with industrial relations and indeed its impact on the economy. It was this probably that defeated the Labour government in 1979 and introduced a Conservative government whose attitude to industrial relations and indeed the economy as a whole was going to be very different.

> Shows how factors interact so cannot be seen in isolation.

> Overall judgement substantiated by foregoing arguments.

This essay would reach Level 5 because it shows very good understanding of the demands of the question. The comments about the failings in industry could be better developed but the essay is analytical, with a balanced argument and well-substantiated judgement in the conclusion.

Changing focus

This essay argues that the most important reason for economic problems was poor industrial relations. But the essay also considers a range of other factors. Pick one of these other factors and rewrite the introduction, the conclusion and the relevant paragraph, arguing that this factor was the most important.

4 The impact of Thatcherism 1979–87

The Thatcher governments

REVISED

Thatcher as leader: character and ideology

Having lost two elections in 1974, Edward Heath resigned as Conservative leader, to be replaced by Margaret Thatcher. Thatcher had embraced fiercely New Right ideas and was determined to avoid the failures of the Heath administration (see Section 3). She was characterised by determination and a reluctance to compromise. Later on in her administration she was accused of being rather arrogant and imperious, factors that contributed to her downfall.

Thatcher was opposed to the post-war consensus and was determined, once elected, to embark on radical change which would see a reduction in the role of government and expansion of the **free market** as the main determinant of economic progress.

However, we must not forget three factors.
● The post-war consensus was already undermined.
● Heath's government had initially adopted similar New Right policies, and Thatcher blamed the subsequent U-turn for the accelerated decline that saw Britain labelled as the 'sick man of Europe'.
● The Labour government had cut expenditure and services in part in response to the IMF loan.

There was therefore some degree to which there was as much continuity as change in Thatcher's policies. However, her overarching policies were to:
● halt Britain's economic decline through the promotion of free market forces
● reduce unnecessary government interference and **bureaucracy**.

Thatcher supported the ideas of the 'Chicago School' of economics, so-called because many of its proponents were based at the University of Chicago. Principal here was the notion of monetarism (see page 64).

Early policies

In her first two years Thatcher seemed to be continuing the policies of her predecessors. She gave British Leyland more subsidies and allowed an above-inflation pay settlement to end a steel strike. However, by 1981 she firmly embarked on New Right economic policies.

Ministers

Thatcher tended to appoint ministers who supported her views – known as 'dries'. Many, such as Norman Tebbit and Nigel Lawson, were self-made men. While she had originally appointed many Heathite **'wets'** they tended to be replaced with **'dries'** as she grew in confidence.

Northern Ireland and the Troubles

Thatcher adopted a hard line against terrorism but sought to extend co-operation between the UK and the Irish Republic in the hope of reaching an eventual settlement.

Attitudes to terrorism

● She was unmoved by IRA prisoners including Bobby Sands starving themselves to death in the hope of gaining the status of prisoners of war while in prison in 1981.
● She was impervious to threats. In 1984 the IRA tried to assassinate her by bombing Brighton's Grand Hotel at which the Conservative Party conference was being held.
● Terrorist violence continued, notably with bombings in 1987 at a Remembrance Day ceremony in Enniskillen, while in 1988 members of the SAS executed three IRA personnel who had been planning terrorist activities in Gibraltar.

Anglo–Irish Agreement 1985

Despite her hard line against terrorists, Thatcher nevertheless signed this agreement as a prelude to greater co-operation between the UK and the Irish Republic.
● The Irish Republic recognised for the first time that Northern Ireland was part of the UK.
● The British Government recognised civil rights for all citizens of Northern Ireland whatever their denomination.

Spectrum of importance

Below are a sample exam-style question and a list of general points that could be used to answer the question. Use your own knowledge and the information on the opposite page to reach a judgement about the importance of these general points to the question posed. Write numbers on the spectrum below to indicate their relative importance. Having done this, write a brief justification of your placement, explaining why some of these factors are more important than others. The resulting diagram could form the basis of an essay plan.

How far did Margaret Thatcher's governments of 1979 and 1983 reflect her support of New Right policies?

1   Mrs Thatcher's Conservative leadership victory

2   The New Right

3   Mrs Thatcher's character and personality

4   Opposition to the post-war consensus

5   Choice of Ministers

6   Early policies

← Least important ———————————————————— Most important →

Develop the detail

Below are a sample exam-style question and a paragraph in answer to this question. The paragraph contains a limited amount of detail. Annotate the paragraph to add additional detail to the answer.

'Margaret Thatcher's policy in Northern Ireland was to be tough on terror but supportive of civil rights.' Assess the validity of this statement.

Thatcher was tough on terror throughout her period in office; she did not respond to demands for prisoner of war status and she did not give in to attacks. IRA members were executed. Despite this, the acts of terrorism continued. She did seek to defend people's civil rights however. She promoted co-operation between Britain and the Republic of Ireland.

Internal Labour divisions and the formation of the SDP

1983 Election

The Conservatives won the 1983 general election with a clear overall majority of 144 seats. While the **'Falklands factor'** was important, the victory was also due in significant part to the disarray within the Labour Party, which lost 3 million votes and saw its share of the vote fall by almost 10 per cent. Indeed the Labour Party was to lose further elections in 1987 and 1992.

Problems for Labour

Following the 1979 electoral defeat, the party leadership moved to the left with the election of Michael Foot. Although well respected by supporters, he lacked the confidence of the electorate.

- The party moreover adopted policies that seemed largely irrelevant to many voters – **unilateral nuclear disarmament**, withdrawal from the EU and greater nationalisation of industry. One senior Labour MP called the 1983 election manifesto the longest suicide note in history.
- Following the memories of industrial unrest in the 1970s, culminating in the winter of discontent, many no longer trusted Labour, associating it very much with the perceived economic decline of that decade.
- The party itself became more democratic with MPs having to seek re-selection by their constituency parties before each election. This gave more power to local activists. However, left-wing groups such as **Militant Tendency** were increasingly gaining influence at local level and pushing through radical socialist agendas, which scared off many moderates.
- The party had split after Foot's election with senior right-wingers leaving to form the new Social Democratic Party (SDP). The most important of these were the so-called 'Gang of Four' – Shirley Williams, Bill Rodgers, Roy Jenkins and David Owen, all of whom had held senior ministerial posts.

The Social Democratic Party

The SDP adopted a moderate, centre line. It supported ideas such as welfare and equal opportunities but opposed policies such as greater nationalisation of industry. Ideologically it was close to the Liberal Party with which it eventually merged.

Although the SDP had enjoyed early electoral successes, the **first past the post system** worked against smaller parties. This was reflected in its alliance with the Liberals in 1983 which saw them gain 25 per cent of the vote but only win 22 seats together. By 1990, the SDP formally merged with the Liberals to form the Liberal Democrats.

Labour reform under Neil Kinnock

Michael Foot resigned after the 1983 electoral defeat. His successor Neil Kinnock understood that left-wing strategies were unpopular with voters and the party needed to reform. At the 1985 party conference he attacked Militant Tendency and asserted that unless the party regained the centre ground it would never again win an election. Members of Militant Tendency were in fact excluded from Labour Party membership and the party did move back to the centre. However, it was a slow process and Mrs Thatcher easily won the 1987 election, albeit with a reduced majority – yet still over 100 seats overall.

Election Results in the Thatcher Years (Numbers of Seats)

Year	Conservatives	Labour	Liberal	Liberal/SDP	Others	Majority
1979	339	269	11		16	43
1983	397	209		23	21	144
1987	375	229		22	24	100

(i) Introducing and concluding an argument

Read the question below and look at the key points of the answer. How good is the proposed introduction? How effective is the proposed conclusion? How could either be improved to achieve a Level 5? Use the mark scheme on page 7 to help you.

How important is the disarray of the other political parties in explaining the electoral victory of Mrs Thatcher in 1983?

Key points
- Falklands factor
- Problems in the Labour Party – left-wing policies such as unilateral nuclear disarmament
- Labour split – growth of SDP
- 'First past the post' electoral system

Introduction

There is some evidence that Thatcher was lucky in that the Labour Party was in considerable disarray. It had moved to the left and adopted policies such as unilateral nuclear disarmament, which many electors found irrelevant. They still distrusted them moreover for their problems in the 1970s such as the winter of discontent. Labour had in fact split, with a new centre party, the Social Democrats, being formed in 1981. However, the British electoral system of 'first past the post' works against new parties, where the party with the majority wins the seat however narrow the victory. Thatcher was moreover helped by her own successes notably over the Falklands campaign of 1982. Therefore in assessing the reasons for her electoral victory we need to examine Conservative strengths as well as opposition weaknesses.

Conclusion

In conclusion, Thatcher was successful in the 1983 election because of the disarray of her political opponents.

(i) Eliminate irrelevance   a

Below are a sample exam-style question and a paragraph written in answer to this question. Read the paragraph and identify those parts of it that are not directly relevant to the question. Draw a line through the information that is irrelevant and justify your deletions in the margin.

'The differences in political policies between the political parties grew much sharper in Britain between 1979 and 1983.' How far do you agree with this statement?

The differences in political policies grew after the ending of the post-war consensus which had seen a broad agreement on areas such as nationalisation and the importance of the welfare state. Mrs Thatcher was particularly scathing of Edward Heath who had conducted policy changes during his administration. She herself was an adherent of the ideas of the New Right, less government interference and expansion of the free market. Labour meanwhile had lurched to the left and advocated greater nationalisation, withdrawal from the EEC and unilateral nuclear disarmament. Its leader Michael Foot was not seriously viewed as a potential prime minister while many still blamed the Labour Party for the failures of the 1970s, especially the winter of discontent, and feared a vote for Labour would see the return of union power. The Labour Party moreover had split, with the SDP being created on a moderate platform such as continued support for the EEC.

Thatcher's economic policies and their impact

Thatcher's economic policies were influenced by the New Right.

Monetarism

Monetarism was associated in particular with the ideas of Chicago economist Milton Friedman. It held that inflation was the greatest economic ill, and governments should increase the value of money by reducing its supply. The more valuable money was the more it could buy, so prices fell. This could be achieved by reducing public spending and increasing rates of interest to deter lending and credit.

Monetarism was applied by raising interest rates and supplying less money. However, it had human costs, noticeably unemployment as weaker firms, which could no longer afford to borrow, went bankrupt. During the early years of the Thatcher government inflation fell from 19 per cent in 1979 to 5 per cent by 1983. However, unemployment rose by 1 million, and there was considerable social unrest including riots in many cities.

U-turns

The first year had been characterised by U-turns – Thatcher's government had allowed high pay rises for steel workers and miners, subsidised the failing nationalised car manufacturer British Leyland and seen inflation rise by 19 per cent. Many felt the Government would go the same way as Heath's.

Economic problems

Many felt Thatcher's economic policies were failing. The cabinet itself was split into 'wets' and 'dries' according to their level of support. At the 1980 Conservative Party conference she asserted the monetarist policies would continue: 'You turn if you want to; the lady's not for turning.'

1981 Budget

Chancellor of the Exchequer Geoffrey Howe introduced a monetarist budget in 1981 which cut government expenditure, increased taxes and took £4 billion out of the economy. More than 300 leading economists publically called for a U-turn. Many felt the Government would be easily defeated in the next general election.

Economic developments of the second term 1983–87

By the mid-1980s, monetarism became less significant but the economy was stimulated by creating greater demand. This was known as 'supply-side economics' and involved such policies as:

● tax reductions
● extensions of credit
● the demise of union power
● deregulation.

Deregulation

The government sought to reduce its own role, which it believed had led to economic decline. The decade therefore saw the abolition of credit controls, deregulation of transport enabling the formation of more private transport companies, and public institutions such as hospitals and schools taking more control of their own finances. The emphasis was overwhelmingly on the development of the free market.

In 1986, Chancellor Nigel Lawson deregulated the Stock Exchange which had been operated according to complex old customs and conventions. With a lack of regulation as to practices and computers making instant transactions possible, London became a centre of world finance.

Privatisation

One key policy was privatisation. The intention was to collect revenue for government from **popular capitalism**, where ordinary people could own shares in private companies. Hence British Airways, Steel, Telecom and Gas were sold off, with priority given to small-scale private investors. The Government raised £7,000 million in 1988–89 – but most of the target investors sold off their shares relatively quickly.

The economy was also advantaged by the production of North Sea gas and oil with revenue approaching 15 per cent of national income by 1985.

(i) Recommended reading

- Recommended reading for Thatcher's economic policies and their impact
- Graham Goodlad, *Thatcher*, pages 59–81, 139–146 (2016)
- Charles Moore, *Margaret, Thatcher: The Authorised Biography*, Vol 1, pages 519–552, 623–656 (2013)
- Richard Vinen, *Thatcher's Britain*, pages 101–134, 178–209 (2009)

(i) Developing an argument

Below are a sample A-level exam-style question, a list of key points to be made in the essay and a paragraph from the essay. Read the question, the plan and the sample paragraph. Rewrite the paragraph in order to develop an argument. The paragraph should answer the question directly and set out the evidence that supports your argument. Crucially it should support an argument by setting out a general answer to the question and reasons that support this.

How accurate is it to say that promotion of the free market was the principal economic strategy of Mrs Thatcher's government between 1979 and 1990?

Key points

- New Right economic ideas – less government intervention in the economy
- Early U-turns on government intervention but no more after 1980
- Monetarist budget 1981 took £8 million out of the economy
- Supply-side economics to create greater demand and stimulate the free market
- Deregulation and privatisation – abolition of controls to favour the free market

Sample paragraph

The Government sought to reduce its own role in the economy, which it believed had led to economic decline. The decade therefore saw the abolition of credit controls, deregulation of transport enabling the formation of more private transport companies, and public institutions such as hospitals and schools taking more control of their own finances. The emphasis was overwhelmingly on the development of the free market.

One key policy was privatisation. The intention was to generate revenue for the Government from the initial sales and popular capitalism, where ordinary people could own shares in private companies. Hence British Airways, Steel, Telecom and Gas were sold off, with priority given to small-scale private investors.

The impact of Thatcherism on society

Divisiveness of policies

Mrs Thatcher's government generally had a divisive impact on society, with many groups benefitting and others becoming hostile and alienated.

Sale of council homes

One of the most popular Thatcher measures of popular capitalism was the selling of council houses to their tenants. The idea was that home owners would have more stake in society. The decision to sell council houses to tenants raised £18 billion as 1.24 million homes were sold. The downside, however, was a shortage of public sector stock as many of the tenants taking advantage of the scheme could have bought new homes on the open market.

Miners' strike 1984–85

The early years of Thatcher's second administration were dominated by the miners' strike. While Thatcher called for the closure of unprofitable pits, pit closures had in fact been taking place for over twenty years – another example of continuity rather than change.

Nevertheless the issue was largely seen in terms of the breaking of union power. The National Union of Miners (NUM) had recently elected a left-winger, Arthur Scargill, as their new president: Scargill had largely been responsible for organising the **flying pickets** in the 1972 dispute. Thatcher meanwhile appointed Ian McGregor as Chairman of the **National Coal Board (NCB)** with a brief to modernise the industry and shut down unprofitable pits: McGregor had already done a similar job as head of British Steel.

The scene was set for bitter confrontation. Many pit areas were in close-knit communities where almost all local men worked in the mines; in the absence of alternative forms of employment, closure would have a devastating effect.

The NUM called for industrial action without the formal ballot that its leaders feared they would lose.

The miners however failed in their battle with the Government.
- Employment Acts in the early 1980s had reduced the power of the unions: **mass picketing** and the **closed shop** were now illegal, and strikes had to be voted for in a formal ballot.
- The Government was stockpiling coal for emergencies.
- The Government chose the time for confrontation – closures were set for the spring and summer months when demand for coal was at its lowest, so any industrial action in protest would also have to take place then.
- The Government was prepared to use the law, both in terms of police action against strikers and using the courts to freeze union assets, as the strike was illegal.
- The strike was never solid and some areas, noticeably Nottinghamshire, refused to join. As the strike dragged on and mining families faced real hardships, miners drifted back to work until in January 1985 the strike was called off.

The Government had won a notable victory and union power declined. There were other struggles.
- Print workers struck against modernisation in 1986, as computer technology was making their typesetting skills redundant.
- TV technicians were dismissed by the TV-am franchise in 1987 when they protested against new working conditions.

Workers generally had to come to terms with new conditions largely as a result of modernisation and technical developments that saw the demise of manual production.

Judgements on the value of a source

Read Source A concerning the 1984 miners' strike and the alternative answers below that assess the value of the source. Which answer will gain the highest level in the mark scheme on page 7? Explain why.

> This source is valuable because it reflects the concern members of the Government felt about the intimidation working miners faced. It also tells us of the debate on the issue in Parliament and shows that the Home Secretary was barracked for his views.

> The source is taken from *The Times* newspaper; therefore it must be reliable.

> The source is partially reliable because it reflects government concerns about the intimidation faced by working miners. It also shows there was considerable disagreement and debate in the House of Commons with Home Secretary Brittan being attacked for his views. Moreover it also shows the human aspect in the sense of the types of intimidation working miners and their families faced. However, it only covers one side of the issue – it doesn't discuss the behaviour of the police, although this is alluded to in the missing section.

Having made your choice, read Source B and write an answer that mirrors the answer you have chosen as your model.

SOURCE A

From 'Police teams to fight intimidation of working miners', *The Times*, 18 May 1984; Leon Brittan was Home Secretary during the miners' strike – here he is addressing the House of Commons about additional measures being taken to protect working miners

Special teams of detectives are being formed to combat intimidation of working miners and their families, Mr Leon Brittan, the Home Secretary, told MPs yesterday.

Extra uniformed officers are being placed in villages identified as high intimidation areas 'patrolling on foot throughout the day and increasing levels of activity during the high risk periods,' he said.

Miners are being encouraged to report all incidents 'with the assurance by the police that they will be investigated and wherever possible charges brought.'

[Brittan responds to criticisms of the drafting into the Midlands coalfield of 1,200 police by left-wing MP Dennis Skinner]

'I want to hear you condemning those who damage property, those who daub paint and those who engage in violent activity on a massive scale.'

The daubing of paint on doors and windows and throwing it over a litter of kittens, killing one, was barbaric, Mr Brittan said.

SOURCE B

From an interview for *The News of the World* given by Mrs Thatcher to journalist Paul Potts, 20 May 1984

We will not let violence win the day.

I think the violence we have seen is appalling. It has done the miners a lot of harm.

We have all got to condemn violence and intimidation. I want every miner, every steelworker, every trade union member, every citizen to do it.

Violence and intimidation are un-British and unacceptable. I believe society is now saying this. It is fed up with them.

I also think there are many, many miners who are not at work and who would like to be at work who are appalled at what has happened and they will be saying don't use violence, use the ballot box.

There is a silent majority in the coalfields of Britain who are being intimidated out of going to work.

It does take a lot of courage to walk through picket lines, particularly if they feel they are being intimidated back in the villages, in their homes.

It also calls for a lot of courage from their families. But we will not let violence and intimidation win the day.

Extra-parliamentary opposition

The Thatcher years were marked by protests over political, economic and social policies, many of which became violent.

Environmentalism

People had increasingly been concerned about threats to the environment since the 1960s. Friends of the Earth had been founded in 1969 and Greenpeace in 1971. They helped draw attention to prominent issues of the time such as global warming and the thinning of the ozone layer in addition to over-exploitation of finite resources. The membership of Friends of the Earth grew from 15,000 to 19,000 during the 1980s and Greenpeace from 30,000 to 40,000.

Britain saw practical support for environmentalism more at the local level – in recycling schemes, for example. However, one major national concern was the perceived ill-effects of nuclear power and especially nuclear weapons. Protests against nuclear weapons had begun in earnest in 1957, after the formation of the Campaign for Nuclear Disarmament (CND). The first of the protest marches to the Atomic Weapons Research Institute at Aldermaston took place in Easter 1958; these marches were to become a feature of the late 1950s and early 1960s. While protests against nuclear weapons and nuclear power continued throughout the period, they developed particularly in the early 1980s, with the deployment of US cruise missiles in Britain. While there were mass protests in London in 1981 and 1983, the opposition in the 1980s came to focus on the Greenham Common peace camp.

Greenham Common

The anti-nuclear weapons movements in Britain took on a new urgency in the late 1970s with the deployment of US Cruise-Pershing II missiles within the UK. In August 1981 protest marchers decided to make a permanent camp outside the RAF base Greenham Common in Berkshire where missiles were sited.

Although the original protesters had included men, it was decided in February 1982 that the camps would be female only. The protests focused on the destructive power of mankind to destroy life on earth by nuclear weapons. Many women saw it as a gender issue: women nurtured the children whose lives might be destroyed by such weapons.

The camps polarised many people: thousands visited to offer support while many were vehemently opposed. Some local people protested about the falling value of their homes and the intrusion of the protestors. Many women were arrested and imprisoned for offences such as vandalism of the perimeter fencing.

The Greenham Common protests continued until the early 21st century.

Poll tax

Mrs Thatcher believed local councils should be more accountable to their electors. She felt if all adults contributed equally to local authority taxes they would be more critical about how money was spent. She therefore introduced a poll tax that all adults would pay – a **flat rate tax** based on individuals rather than an unequal one based on householders. The new policy was introduced first in Scotland in April 1989 to huge opposition. It was found that most people were paying far more than previously through the rates and the biggest burden fell on the poorest – while the tax cost two and a half times as much to collect. Indeed, some suggested it cost more to collect than it raised.

When the tax was spread to England and Wales, there was even more opposition with significant marches and protests – for example, at Trafalgar Square on 31 March 1990 – and many simply refusing to pay.

The poll tax outlasted Mrs Thatcher but was abandoned in 1991, to be replaced by a council tax, similar to the old rating system.

Judgements on the value of a source   a

Read Source A and the alternative answers below that assess the value of the source. Which answer will gain the highest level in the mark scheme on page 7? Explain why.

> As Caroline Blackwood is in sympathy with the women on Greenham Common, the source is clearly biased and this limits its value. It says a lot about their noble aims to prevent nuclear war.

> This source is useful for explaining the aims of the women at Greenham Common and the petty attitudes of the local council in trying to disperse them. Indeed it raises a contrast between the small-minded approach of the local council and the high ideals behind the camp.

> This source is in part useful in that it is a piece of contemporary journalism in which Blackwood attempts to explain the motives of the women at Greenham Common at the time. However, clearly she is biased in how she contrasts the noble aspirations of the women with the pettiness of the local council. She does not explain the council's motives. The provenance itself could limit its utility as evidence. Clearly she is biased in the women's favour, talking of 'helpless anger', their being 'the voice of people all over the world.' This makes the protest seem high minded. However, it is asserted with no evidence in support.

Having made your choice, read Source B and write an answer that mirrors the answer above that you have chosen as your model.

SOURCE A

From Caroline Blackwood, *On the Perimeter*; Blackwood was a journalist who regularly visited and wrote about the Greenham Common camps – she was in sympathy with the aims of the women

When Newbury council tried to scare them away from the missile base by threatening to seize their plastic cups and their tea bags, it was a very small minded approach to human beings who felt they were already facing the unendurable, for they foresaw the inevitable destruction of their children.

It was the acceptance that they were helpless to change the destructive course of all governments who ignored the misery and unemployment of their people as they sunk the financial resources of the nation into death dealing weapons that had made these women angry. It was a helpless anger that had given them the courage to put up a symbolic fight. If nothing was to be gained by their struggle, they knew certainly that nothing could be lost. By their symbolic presence on Greenham Common, they hoped to act as the voice of the millions of people all over the world who recognised that they had no voice.

SOURCE B

Anti-CND campaign memo from Lord Beloff concerning the Greenham Common women, dated 15 December 1982; Lord Beloff was a government adviser.

[W]e must abandon the kid-gloves approach and seek publically to discredit the Greenham Common women and their supporters in the country. Ministers must stop prefacing their speeches with tributes to their fine motives and tender consciences. This just helps to build them up. To do the reverse we need two kinds of intelligence and ministers should brief our intelligence services accordingly.

First we must get and produce evidence of the sources of the movement's finance. We know from cases on the Continent that in a number of countries money has passed directly from Soviet embassies to the peace movements. It may be that it has been successfully 'laundered' here or perhaps it comes from Gadaffi or other anti-western sources. It is clear the amounts involved have not been subscribed in full by bona-fide British citizens.

Second we need proper investigation of the background and characters of the Greenham Common women: a clean bill of health from the local police is not enough. None appear to be from the locality itself. We need to know more of their political and personal backgrounds so that the aura of martyrdom can be stripped from them.

Foreign affairs: the Falklands, the Cold War and attitudes towards Europe

The Falklands campaign 1982

Background to the conflict

The Falklands are a series of rocky islands off the coast of Argentina. Britain had possessed them since 1833, but Argentina claimed them too. In April 1982, the Argentine military invaded the islands.

The conflict

The British military leaders assured Mrs Thatcher they could win the islands back. A task force therefore sailed on 8 April and began to bomb Argentine positions on the Falklands.

The United Nations and leaders of the USA tried to arrange a peaceful solution. On 2 May a British submarine sank the Argentinian cruiser *Belgrano* with the loss of hundreds of lives. This action ended efforts to broker peace.

The subsequent conflict continued until June when the Falklands capital Port Stanley was captured and the Argentinian forces surrendered. However, victory was achieved at the loss of 255 British and 665 Argentinian lives. It may be that the victory helped to restore British confidence – but it certainly enhanced the position of Thatcher.

Europe

It was disagreements over Europe that led directly to the downfall of Thatcher (see page 74). By the late 1980s she was concerned both about the waste and inefficiency, and the threat to British sovereignty from closer union, as more powers were devolved to the European Union (EU). She supported economic ties but baulked at greater political union. While she had accepted the Single Europe Act in 1985, which emphasised closer ties, she was reluctant to see them implemented. This came to a head over the issue of currency exchange rates.

Exchange Rate Mechanism

The EU had the ultimate goal of a single currency. As a precursor to this the **Exchange Rate Mechanism (ERM)** was a scheme by which the values of the currencies of member states would be pegged to the strongest – the Deutschmark. This would keep the prices of exports artificially high.

Britain and the Cold War

Thatcher was an avowed anti-Communist who was nicknamed 'The Iron Lady'. She got on particularly well with President Reagan of the USA who shared her prejudice: both felt the USSR was 'an evil empire'. As a result, Thatcher was a stalwart ally of the USA during the 1980s. She supported in particular the Polish trade union movement Solidarity, which was denouncing the Communist government, and visited Eastern European countries to considerable acclaim. She supported the reformist leader of the USSR, Mikhail Gorbachev, and encouraged his attempts to modernise his country.

Thatcher enjoyed considerable respect on the international stage and has been praised as a key figure in the ending of the Cold War. She is judged far less critically in the USA and former Communist bloc than in the UK.

Analyse the answer

Read Source A and the paragraph below that analyses it.

Highlight:
- the sections that refer to content and incorporate knowledge
- the sections that refer to provenance
- the sections that refer to tone and emphasis.

> This source is useful because it shows a private correspondence from Thatcher's ally President Reagan of the USA, where the president can be more informal and perhaps frank in his comments. Here we see an observation about the intractability of the Argentinian leader General Galtieri combined with personal thanks for making the US envoy welcome. This hints at a close relationship between Thatcher and Reagan. This is supported too by the first paragraph, which suggests the two leaders could have a personal discussion next morning. There is clearly a close relationship between the two. The letter does also however suggest Galtieri was in a difficult position, and feared any conflict with Britain would harm his relations with the USA. The letter is useful in showing that the US position was itself difficult in having two close allies on the brink of war. While Reagan recognised that Britain was one of his closest allies, he also acknowledged common ground and interests with Argentina. In this sense the source is very useful in showing how the USA fervently sought a negotiated settlement — which is presumably why Reagan sent his Secretary of State between Britain and Argentina in an attempt to broker peace.

SOURCE A

Letter from President Reagan to Margaret Thatcher, dated 15 April 1982; Reagan's Secretary of State, General Al Haig, was trying to reach a negotiated settlement between Britain and Argentina about the Falklands Crisis

Dear Margaret,

At his request, I have just talked with General Galtieri concerning the Falklands Islands Crisis. I wanted to relay to you a summary of that conversation. In view of the late hour in London, I have sent you this message but we can talk on the telephone tomorrow morning if you think it is necessary.

General Galtieri reaffirmed his desire to avoid conflict with your country and his fears that conflict would cause deterioration of recently improving relations with the United States. He said that the advance of your fleet and the blockade of the Islands were making his situation difficult. ... General Galtieri promised to deal honestly and seriously with Secretary Haig.

I would like to add we greatly appreciate the hospitality you have shown to Al during his two visits. We are also grateful for the receptivity you have shown to our efforts to find a common ground between your country, one of our closest allies, and Argentina with whom we would like to be able to cooperate in advancing specific interests in this hemisphere.

Warm Regards

Ron

From the White House to the Cabinet Office

Secret via Cabinet Office channels

 Recommended reading

- Linda Christmas, *Chopping Down the Cherry Trees* (pieces of journalism) (1989)
- Andy McSmith, *No Such Thing as Society*, pages 1–34, 152–171, 319–335 (2011)
- A.N. Wilson, *Our Times*, pages 271–307 (2008)

Exam focus

Below is a sample Level 5 answer to an A-level essay question. Read it and the comments around it.

To what extent was society divided by the social and economic policies of the Conservative government 1979 to 1990?

The Conservative Party under Margaret Thatcher won the 1979 election committed to the ideas of 'New Right' thinking such as less state interference and promotion of free market forces. Although the post-war consensus had already been undermined, this was widely seen as a new departure and many of the policies undertaken were felt to be divisive within society. However, some policies such as the sale of council houses and promotion of popular capitalism were widely popular while in other respects the Government simply responded to changes taking place in society and the economy. In investigating the divisive nature of policies it is important to note that it depends on which groups were affected and also how new the policies were.

> Introduction shows the full range of question.

Thatcher's overarching policies were: to halt Britain's economic decline through the promotion of free market forces; and to reduce unnecessary government interference and bureaucracy. One significant policy here was monetarism. This held that inflation was the greatest economic ill, and governments should increase the value of money by reducing its supply. The more valuable money was the more it could buy so prices were lower. This could be achieved by reducing public spending and increasing rates of interest to deter lending and credit. However, it had human costs, noticeably unemployment as weaker firms, which could no longer afford to borrow, went bankrupt. During the early years of the Thatcher government, inflation fell from 19 per cent in 1979 to 5 per cent by 1983. However, unemployment rose by 1 million, and there was considerable social unrest including riots in many cities. This was clearly divisive. Many indeed felt Thatcher's economic policies were failing. The cabinet itself was split. Chancellor of the Exchequer Geoffrey Howe had introduced a monetarist budget in 1981 which cut government expenditure, increased taxes and took £4 billion out of the economy. Over 300 leading economists publically called for a U-turn. Many felt the Government would be easily defeated in the next general election. That it wasn't had more to do with the disarray of the opposition and the 'Falklands factor' than widespread support for Conservative economic policies.

> Shows how factors interact and maintains question focus.

By the mid-1980s, monetarism became less significant but the economy was stimulated by creating greater demand. This was known as 'supply-side economics' and involved such policies as: tax reductions, extensions of credit, the demise of union power, reducing welfare benefits and deregulation. Here the Government sought to reduce its own role which it believed had led to economic decline. This involved the abolition of credit controls, deregulation of transport enabling the formation of more private transport companies, and public institutions such as hospitals and schools taking more control of their own finances. The emphasis was overwhelmingly on the development of the free market. The economy was improving, however, and the Government took credit. More people began to actively support the Government, particularly in its anti-union legislation which ended the industrial unrest of the previous decade by outlawing such practices as secondary picketing and sympathy strikes and insisting on formal ballots before a strike could be called. Also significant was the promotion of popular capitalism.

> Strikes a balance in terms of question.

One key policy allied to the latter was privatisation. The intention was to secure revenue for Government from the initial sales where ordinary people could own shares in private companies. Hence British Airways, Steel, Telecom and Gas were sold off, with priority given to small-scale private investors. The Government raised £7,000 million in 1988–89 – but most of the target investors sold off their shares relatively quickly. The sale of council houses to their

Quick quizzes at **www.hoddereducation.co.uk/myrevisionnotes**

tenants was one of the most popular measures of Thatcher's view of popular capitalism. The idea was that home owners would have more stake in society. The decision to sell council houses to tenants raised £18 billion as 1.24 million homes were sold. The downside however was a shortage of public sector housing stock as many of the tenants taking advantage of the scheme could have bought new homes on the open market.

Useful material in support without overwhelming the argument

However, society remained in many ways divided, as exemplified by the miners' strike of 1984–85. Many coal mines were largely unprofitable and running at a loss. While Thatcher called for the closure of unprofitable pits, this process had already begun – another example of continuity rather than change. Nevertheless the issue was largely seen in terms of the breaking of union power. The scene was set for bitter confrontation. Many pit areas were close-knit communities where almost all local men worked in the mines; in the absence of alternative forms of employment, closure would have a devastating effect. The Government chose the time for confrontation – closures were set for the spring and summer months when demand for coal was at its lowest, so any industrial action in protest would also have to take place then. It was also prepared to use the full weight of the law, both in terms of police action against strikers and using the courts to freeze union assets, as the strike was illegal.

Attempts a balance but shows government determination to win.

The Government had won a notable victory and union power was on the decline in all areas. However, this was also in part a result of changes in technology and industrial methods which meant many traditional skills were no longer necessary. In particular, as heavy industry, which had the highest concentrations of union membership, declined, patterns of employment would have changed irrespective of the Government and so while this was undoubtedly a decisive factor, it cannot necessarily be blamed on government policy.

Return to wider argument in this case to put factor into context.

However, many see the poll tax as a real example of division within society. The 'poll tax' was designed to replace the local authority rating system based on the size of properties with a community charge equally divided among all adults in a specific authority. The new policy was introduced first in Scotland to huge opposition. It was found that most people were paying far more and the biggest burden fell on the poorest. When the tax was spread to England and Wales, there was even more opposition with significant marches, protests – for example, at Trafalgar Square on 31 March – and many refusing to pay.

Overall, while many Conservative policies may have been divisive, it is also true that society itself was changing and those changes themselves would have resulted in division whether the Conservatives under Thatcher had been the Government or not. The promotion of free market forces and lack of support for failing industries recognised economic realities, for example, and to have supported them may only have put off the inevitable decline. While there was human cost, this would have come eventually whether Thatcher was in power or not. However, some policies, notably the poll tax and the responses to the miners' strike, did result in conflict within society. To some extent Thatcher was simply developing policies already in place such as government retrenchment. In terms of popular capitalism, some benefited and others didn't. However, all governments initiate policies that advantage some groups over others. If Thatcher's government was divisive, therefore, all governments are to a certain extent. It may be that hers was more divisive than most, but society was changing and many of her policies reflected those changes.

Balanced conclusion based on discriminating use of evidence.

Judgement supported by balanced argument.

This is clearly a Level 5 answer that attempts to strike a balance. It is well organised and the judgement is substantively supported by argument and analysis.

Consolidation

This is a long and detailed essay. Without losing the overall argument of the essay, experiment with reducing its length by 100 words. This a useful exercise for trying to produce an essay that gets to the heart of the question without being overlong.

5 Towards a new consensus 1987–97

The fall of Thatcher and her legacy REVISED

Margaret Thatcher won a third term of office in 1987. Although her majority was reduced it was still 100. Perhaps this made her too confident; colleagues felt she was becoming too arrogant and dominating. Her final term of office was beset with controversy and quarrelling within the Government. Thatcher had made too many enemies among her erstwhile friends.

Problems with the Government

The Westland Affair 1986

Westland was a British helicopter company in financial difficulties. Thatcher favoured it being taken over by an American company while her Defence Secretary Michael Heseltine supported a European consortium. When the prime minister overrode him, he stormed out of the cabinet.

Poll tax, or community charge

Thatcher insisted on the introduction of this policy despite protests from her colleagues about its unpopularity and impracticability.

Resignation of Nigel Lawson

Lawson had been successful as Chancellor, presiding over Britain's economic growth and deregulation. Lawson however resigned when he believed Thatcher was paying more attention to her economic advisers such as Alan Walters than to him.

Resignation of Sir Geoffrey Howe

Thatcher had been unenthusiastic about closer ties within the EU but allowed herself to be persuaded about the benefits of joining the Exchange Rate Mechanism, which tied members' currencies closer together. However, she increasingly made her opposition to closer integration known. In October 1990, for example, she asserted that Britain would never join a single European currency, and, to calls for greater political integration, responded 'No! No! No!'

It was this that led to the resignation of her Deputy Prime Minister Sir Geoffrey Howe, whose dignified resignation speech had a tinge of sadness as he said his efforts were constantly being undermined by his prime minister.

A series of by-election defeats in 1990 led to Michael Heseltine standing against her in a leadership contest. A narrow victory in the first round convinced her she might not win the second and she resigned. The Thatcher era was over.

Thatcher: an assessment of her legacy

When Thatcher was asked in retirement what she had changed, she replied 'Everything'. This was, however, an exaggeration. She undoubtedly brought a new respect back to Britain, destroyed the power of trade unions and developed the free market. Policies such as the sale of council houses were genuinely popular. However, she did not reduce the role of government – indeed it increased as privatised industries faced greater accountability and regulation. She failed to reduce the cost of the welfare state – this increased through greater numbers of unemployed requiring benefits. She did not interfere with the National Health Service or other social services. Britain did not withdraw from Europe – indeed, albeit reluctantly, she accepted the ERM.

Monetarism was abandoned. Britain lost 25 per cent of its manufacturing base and the average growth rate was 1.75 per cent, less than during the years of Labour which Thatcher had so castigated. Britain's trade deficit grew as did unemployment, while the gap between rich and poor grew exponentially; according to the Rowntree Trust, the incomes of the top 10 per cent rose by more than 50 per cent while those of lowest earners actually fell.

Like all administrations, Thatcher's was a mix of success and failure.

Analyse the answer ⓐ

Read the source and the paragraph provided that analyses it.

Highlight in the answer:

- the sections that refer to content and incorporate knowledge
- the sections that refer to provenance
- the sections that refer to tone and emphasis.

This source is immediate, a reported speech in the House of Commons. Deputy Prime Minister Sir Geoffrey Howe resigned over Mrs Thatcher's attitude to Europe, which he believed had undermined his own position particularly when negotiating over issues such as the Exchange Rate Mechanism. For Howe, one of Mrs Thatcher's most loyal supporters who had served throughout her term of office, initially during her first administration as Chancellor, to attack her leadership in such a way must have shocked many in the House. It is also useful in terms of tone and emphasis. One can almost hear the sadness behind the incredulity. He is saying it is impossible for him to do his job effectively with a leader who almost casually dismisses the case he is arguing with European partners. Also the cricketing allegory was well chosen in that it would be easily understood by anyone with any slight knowledge of the sport. Howe moreover goes on to widen the argument to explain how difficult it is for British businessmen when their potential clients have an image of a finger-wagging prime minister. The implication is that they become prejudiced against Britain because of Mrs Thatcher and the image she portrays.

SOURCE A

Extract from Sir Geoffrey Howe's resignation speech in the House of Commons, 13 November 1989

It was remarkable – indeed, it was tragic – to hear my Right Honourable Friend dismissing, with such personalised incredulity, the very idea that the Hard ECU proposal might find growing favour among the peoples of Europe, just as it was extraordinary to hear her assert that the whole idea of EMU might be open for consideration only by future generations. Those future generations are with us today. How on earth are the Chancellor and the Governor of the Bank of England, commending the Hard ECU as they strive to, to be taken as serious participants in the debate against that kind of background noise? I believe that both the Chancellor and the Governor are cricketing enthusiasts, so I hope that there is no monopoly of cricketing metaphors. It is rather like sending your opening batsmen to the crease only for them to find, the moment the first balls are bowled, that their bats have been broken before the game by the team captain.

The point was perhaps more sharply put by a British businessman, trading in Brussels and elsewhere, who wrote to me last week, stating:

'People throughout Europe see our Prime Minister's finger-wagging and hear her passionate, "No, No, No", much more clearly than the content of the carefully worded formal texts.'

John Major's government 1990–97

John Major's government was to face continuous crises over **sleaze** and membership of the EU – but it started well.

Change and continuity

Major's main task was to develop Thatcher's legacy and unite the Conservative Party in order to retain power. Indeed it was to create a new consensus based on Thatcher's policies of the free market and people taking responsibility for their own lives with support for the most vulnerable. However, Major broke with some elements of Thatcherism.

● More was spent on healthcare and education.
● Britain signed the 1992 Maastricht Treaty developing closer ties within the EEC.

Poll tax

The unpopular poll tax was withdrawn to be replaced by a council tax according to eight bands of property value.

Citizen's Charter

This was introduced in 1991 to offer guarantees about public service and the rights and responsibilities of citizens.

Problems in government 1992–97

Major won the 1992 election with an overall majority of 22. After this, however, the Government faced continuous problems.

Sleaze

Major's administration was rocked by a series of scandals involving illicit sex and/or corruption. This again lost the Government credibility – particularly as Major had campaigned for a 'return to basics', by which he meant self-responsibility and moral values. The campaign seemed hollow.

Major's government came increasingly under attack by the media and was ridiculed by satirical programmes such as *Spitting Image*.

Economic developments

The early years of the Major government were dominated by the fallout from 'Black Wednesday'.

ERM and Black Wednesday

The ERM tied the value of European currencies to the most successful – the Deutschmark. The value of the £ was DM 2.95. Many felt this was overpriced. In September 1992 international bankers began to sell sterling so its market value fell. To maintain the exchange rate of £1 to DM 2.95, Chancellor Norman Lamont raised interest rates to 15 per cent and sold £30 billion of British foreign reserves. This was insufficient – on 'Black Wednesday', 16 September 1992, Britain had to withdraw from the ERM.

In the short term this seemed disastrous for Britain. Its international credibility was undermined. The **Eurosceptics** among Major's government became even more disillusioned with membership of the EU. Many lost faith in the Government's handling of the economy.

In the longer term, however, the withdrawal worked to Britain's advantage. Finding its own market level, the £ began to recover and indeed by 1996 was valued at DM 3 – higher than in the days of the ERM. The economy itself began to thrive with Britain's growth rate higher than the EU average.

Northern Ireland

Major sought an end to the conflict, in which the violence continued.
● In 1990, the IRA mortar-bombed 10 Downing Street although luckily no one was hurt.
● In 1993 an IRA bombing in the Cheshire town of Warrington saw two children killed.

However, some agreements were reached.
● In 1993 the Downing Street Declaration asserted that Britain had no selfish interest in Northern Ireland.
● The Declaration affirmed that the inhabitants of Northern Ireland should vote on their own future.

In August 1994 the IRA declared a ceasefire. US negotiator George Mitchell tried to broker a lasting peace. When his efforts failed, the ceasefire ended – but progress was nevertheless being made behind the scenes.

Judgements on the value of a source

Read Source A and the alternative answers below that assess the value of the source in terms of provenance.

Which answer will gain the highest level in the mark scheme on page 7? Explain why.

> This source is partly useful because it was published fairly soon after the Downing Street Declaration, although we don't know when the interviews and research on which Tooley bases his judgements were conducted. Clearly while there is no indication he had IRA sympathies, he does show admiration for their tenacity, and this partiality may have limited the usefulness of the source in terms of objectivity. Having said this, the source is taken from a work intending to show the Republican mindset so in this instance objectivity may not be as significant a factor in assessing usefulness.

> This is a piece of reportage. Reporters should always seek to be objective and try to arrive at the truth of a case through investigation. Clearly this reporter has done a lot of research to arrive at his conclusions.

> This source is very useful because the author was clearly there at the time and his book dates from the period under consideration. He interviewed hundreds of people to arrive at his conclusions and clearly we need the Republican mindset explained so we can arrive at a full picture of what was going on in Northern Ireland in the 1990s.

Having made your choice, read Source B and write an answer that mirrors the answer above that you have chosen as your model.

SOURCE A

From Kevin Tooley, *Rebel Hearts: Journeys within the IRA's Soul*; Tooley was a journalist who interviewed hundreds of Republicans to explain their mindset

As a philosophy, Irish Republicanism is the unqualified belief that a United Ireland is an intrinsic good, and the demand for Irish national self-determination so pressing, so overwhelming that this goal must be pursued at all costs but principally and immediately by force of arms. Ireland must be reunited and the illegitimate British crown government forced to leave that portion of the country, Northern Ireland, over which it rules and claims jurisdiction. All other political questions and struggles are secondary and inferior to the resolution of the 'national question'.

Outside their Ulster strongholds, the IRA were universally reviled as a terrorist organisation guilty of some of the bloodiest acts in recent political history. It is a faith shared by a band of brothers against impossible odds. ...

But far from weakening the Republican cause these obstacles merely make it all the more formidable and more profound.

SOURCE B

Gusty Spence, a former Protestant gunman, made the announcement of a Protestant paramilitary ceasefire in response to that of the IRA in 1995.

In all sincerity, we offer to the loved ones of all innocent victims over the past 25 years abject and true remorse. No words of ours will compensate for the intolerable suffering they have undergone during the conflict.

Let us firmly resolve to respect our differing views of freedom, culture and aspiration and never again permit our political circumstances to degenerate into bloody warfare.

We are on the threshold of a new and exciting beginning with our battles in the future being political battles, fought on the side of honesty, decency and democracy against the negativity of mistrust, misunderstanding and malevolence, so that together, we can bring forth a wholesome society in which our children and their children, will know the true meaning of peace.

Realignment of the Labour Party under Kinnock, Smith and Blair

In the 1997 General Election, Tony Blair won a small overall majority of 183, winning by 13 percentage points over the Conservatives (44.4 to 31.4 per cent). This was the result both of problems in the Conservative Party and the charisma and expectancy of **'New Labour'**.

Problems in the Conservative Party

- Having governed continuously since 1979, the party was tired and in need of rebuilding.
- The party was split particularly over membership of the EU.
- Despite economic successes many voters still lacked faith in its ability to govern the economy successfully.
- The sleaze allegations had undermined its credibility.

Labour however was vibrant and rejuvenated. The party had reinvented itself since the defeats of the 1980s.

- During the 1980s left-wing elements often associated with the Marxist group Militant Tendency had gained control of many local Labour parties. After the 1983 defeat Michael Foot resigned. His successor, Neil Kinnock, despite being himself associated with the left, began a campaign to expel these forces and introduce more moderate policies. For example, he dropped unilateral nuclear disarmament and became more conciliatory on membership of the EU. Kinnock resigned after successive electoral defeats in 1987 and 1992 but his successor John Smith continued the process he had begun.
- After the unexpected and sudden death of John Smith in 1994, Tony Blair was elected leader with an accelerated reform agenda – New Labour.

New Labour

The natural successors to John Smith were Tony Blair, a charismatic young leader, and Gordon Brown, more dour and taciturn but an organisational genius. Many assert they did a deal over dinner at the Granita restaurant whereby Blair would become party leader but when in power would give Brown control of the economy and stand down in 2003 for Brown to replace him. True or not, New Labour did introduce new policies that conflicted with those of the traditional party.

- Nationalisation, a key Labour policy (Clause 4), was abandoned.
- Business was to be courted to ensure people felt Labour could be trusted with the economy.
- Legal restrictions on unions would be maintained – despite unions being a major source of Labour Party funds.
- Old ideas such as class struggles were felt to be irrelevant.

Presentation of New Labour

Blair was a master of presentation. He employed an array of advisers and public relations experts, also known as 'spin doctors', to sell policies to the public through manipulation of the media. They were also experts of the soundbite – a short pithy phrase that summarised a policy and its importance – for example, 'Tough on crime and tough on the causes of crime', and as a New Labour priority, 'Education, Education, Education'. In addition, he promoted a progressive image in direct contrast to Major's tired, grey government – heading footballs with famous players and being seen with current music stars who would also be invited to functions at 10 Downing Street. This promotion of the so-called **Cool Britannia** resonated with many voters, particularly the younger generation.

RAG – Rate the factors

Below are a sample exam-style question and factors that could be used to answer it. Read the question, study the factors and, using three coloured pens, put a red, amber or green star next to the factors to show:

- red – factors that have no relevance to the question
- amber – factors that have some significance to the question
- green – factors that are directly relevant to the question.

> To what extent was the development of New Labour the most important factor in the Conservative electoral defeat in 1997?

- Mrs Thatcher resigned in 1990
- The Conservatives won the 1992 election
- Labour leader John Smith died in 1994
- The Conservative Party was split over its policies towards the EU
- The Conservative government was harmed over issues of sleaze
- Tony Blair and Gordon Brown may have done a deal at the Granita restaurant
- Tony Blair and Gordon Brown developed New Labour
- The Conservative Party seemed tired and jaded in comparison to New Labour
- Clause 4 was abandoned as a Labour policy
- Tony Blair and his advisers developed the idea of Cool Britannia
- Many celebrities supported Labour in the 1997 election

Now repeat this activity with the following question:

> 'The Conservative Party lost the 1997 election mainly through its own failings.' How far do you agree with this statement?

Develop the detail

Below are a sample exam-style question and a paragraph written in answer to the question. The paragraph contains a limited amount of detail. Annotate the paragraph to add additional detail to the answer.

> How far did Tony Blair and his supporters reform the Labour Party in the period 1994 to 1997?

Tony Blair introduced New Labour. This involved many changes in policy and organisation. Traditional Labour policies such as nationalisation and policies specifically aimed at the promotion of the working classes were abandoned. Links with business were developed. The legislation restricting union activities was continued. New Labour attempted to be fashionable and modern through the promotion of ideas such as 'Cool Britannia'.

Social issues

REVISED

The years when Major was prime minister were characterised by fears that society was under threat from such factors as rising crime, less respect, particularly among the young and less inhibited behaviour. Many people thought society was becoming more violent.

Race relations

In 1995, Bernie Grant, a Labour MP, asserted that most black Britons lacked any future in the UK because of racism. Racist attacks were commonplace but the event that shocked most people was the death of Stephen Lawrence in April 1993. It served to emphasise how many black people were living in fear. In 1997 the Labour government set up the MacPherson Inquiry into the police investigation. This found the investigation had been hampered by **institutional racism** in the Metropolitan Police.

Stephen Lawrence

Stephen Lawrence was a bright, talented black eighteen-year-old who was murdered by a gang of white youths in Eltham, South London, a venue for previous racist attacks. No one was brought to trial even though the suspected perpetrators were quickly identified. The *Daily Mail* indeed identified them and dared them to sue for defamation.

Crime

Crime figures are notoriously hard to gauge, but the perception was that Britain was becoming a more lawless society. This was highlighted by several high-profile murders:

James Bulger

In February 1993 two-year-old James Bulger was abducted and brutally murdered by two young boys from deeply dysfunctional families.

Philip Lawrence

In 1995 Philip Lawrence, a popular head teacher, was murdered by a youth outside his school gates as he tried to break up a fight arising from conflict between different gangs in the area. This crime appeared to symbolise the loss of moral values and respect for authority that seemed to be an overwhelming characteristic of the decade.

Youth

It was feared that young people were becoming more violent. Indeed many older people feared attacks from the young – although it was young people themselves who were most likely to be the victims of violence.

Acid house raves

One new phenomenon was organised 'raves', where masses of young people would descend upon a venue to dance to loud music – acid house. Often they would take a drug new on the market – Ecstasy – which was responsible for several well-publicised deaths. So many young people took Ecstasy that it was felt to be impossible to police. Nevertheless the Government did act to prevent acid house parties that involved trespass and considerable disruption for local communities. The 1994 Criminal Justice and Public Order Act criminalised them although existing Public Order Acts could also be used. In 1990 the Entertainment (Increased Penalties) Act was used to stop a rave at Gildersome, near Leeds, where 800 revellers were arrested.

Similarly, Public Order Acts were used to break up convoys of 'new age travellers' who often descended upon unsuspecting communities or clogged up roads.

The position of women

Women had equal rights in law but still faced a **'glass ceiling'** or discrimination at work, particularly in senior positions. One development in 1994 was the legalisation of women priests.

Many women became more assertive in adopting 'laddish behaviour' and becoming less inhibited sexually, influenced for example by the US TV programme *Sex and the City*. Younger girls listened to the Spice Girls, who acted as role models for 'girl power'.

Turning assertion into argument a

Below are a series of definitions, a sample exam-style question and two sample conclusions. One of the conclusions achieves a high mark because it contains an argument. The other achieves a lower mark because it contains only description and assertion. Identify which is which. The mark scheme on page 7 will help you.

Description: a detailed account

Assertion: a statement of fact or an opinion that is not supported by reason

Reason: a statement that explains or justifies something

Argument: an assertion justified by a reason

How significant were concerns about racism and violence in the 1990s?

Conclusion 1

Overall there were serious concerns about racism and violence. Stephen Lawrence was murdered by a gang of white youths in Eltham in 1993 and no one was convicted even though the suspects were well known and the *Daily Mail* published their identities. The subsequent MacPherson Inquiry found that many of the police themselves had racist attitudes. A series of high-profile murders made many people believe society was becoming more violent. James Bulger was only two years old when he was brutally murdered by two boys.

Conclusion 2

While there were undoubtedly concerns about racism and violence, exacerbated, for example, by the murders of James Bulger and Stephen Lawrence, crime levels remained comparatively low. Both Conservative and Labour governments acted to address issues of racism and violence, for example, setting up the MacPherson Inquiry in 1997, which was unafraid to accuse the Metropolitan Police of institutionalised racism, and passing laws to reduce activities such as illegal raves where antisocial behaviour disrupted communities. One could indeed argue that because people could be shocked by specific crimes, it shows they were comparatively rare. However, this is not to minimise their impact. The concerns were real.

 Moving from assertion to argument

Below are a sample exam-style question and a series of assertions. Read the exam question and then add a justification to each of the assertions to turn it into an argument.

'Crime and violence were major concerns facing the Government during the 1990s.' How far do you agree with this statement?

The murder of Stephen Lawrence became a major national issue in 1993 because

_____

_____

Many people believed Britain was becoming more violent because

_____

_____

_____

The Government introduced more restrictive legislation to prevent antisocial activity because

_____

_____

Social liberalism and anti-establishment culture

Social liberalism

'Social liberalism' refers to a political and social system that attempts a balance between individual liberties and the duties of a citizen. Proponents believe the Government should look after people without stifling their individuality. John Major supported this view through initiatives such as the Citizens' Charter (see page 76), but his period of office also saw a liberalisation of attitudes independent of government interference. In 1990, for example, 69 per cent of respondents felt homosexuality was morally wrong, while ten years later less than 35 per cent felt the same. Indeed during the decade homosexuality was generally accepted within society and comparatively few faced persecution as a result of their sexuality.

Anti-establishment culture

Possibly in tandem with growing social liberalism came greater indifference or indeed hostility to the establishment. This was due to several factors.

- Greater media coverage of establishment figures showed their flaws. This was particularly noticeable in attitudes to the royal family. In 1992, Prince Charles separated from his wife, Princess Diana, and the resultant revelations seemed to do significant harm to the monarchy. This was exacerbated in the subsequent marital break-up of Prince Andrew and his wife, particularly in terms of media coverage of her activities.
- Satirists had a field day with the government's involvement in sleaze and sexual scandals. Salacious gossip, often without any substance, turned those responsible into figures of fun.
- John Major himself was seen as dour and colourless. The puppet that represented him in the popular satirical programme *Spitting Image* was entirely grey – both clothing and complexion.
- People spoke of a laddish culture of poor social behaviour and drunkenness among celebrities who should have acted as more positive role models. The trend was also noticed in girls who indulged in 'ladette' behaviour similar to that of men.

Some commentators felt many people were abandoning politics and any interest in current affairs altogether, simply living for work and pleasure. However, people were still prepared to become actively engaged in causes, for example, in terms of the environment. This was known as 'direct action'.

Newbury protest

The mid-1990s saw protests against the proposed Newbury bypass road. Protestors lived in trees and chained themselves to objects to prevent work going ahead. One teenaged protestor, 'Swampy', became something of a media star and was even given his own column in the *Sunday Mirror* newspaper.

The protests meant the project went 50 per cent over budget and took 34 months to complete. Although the bypass was completed in 1998, there was more local consultation before others were begun.

The National Lottery

The decade also saw what many saw as the development of a culture of greed with the introduction in 1994 of the National Lottery. This proved so successful that a mid-week draw was introduced in 1997, although the chances of winning a jackpot were pitifully small. Nevertheless almost £50 million worth of tickets were bought in the first week and each Saturday night an estimated 22 million tuned in to see the winning balls be shown on TV.

RAG – Rate the factors

Below are a sample exam-style question and a list of factors that could be used to answer the question. Read the question, study the factors and, using three coloured pens, put a red, amber or green star next to the factors to show:

- red – factors that have no relevance to the question
- amber – factors that have some significance to the question
- green – factors that are directly relevant to the question.

How far do you agree that an anti-establishment culture grew in Britain during the period of office of John Major?

- Downfall of Margaret Thatcher
- Growth of satirical programmes such as *Spitting Image*
- Sleaze and scandal in government
- The popularity of the National Lottery
- Laddish behaviour

- Environmental protests and direct action
- Personality of John Major
- Scandals in the royal family
- Growth of media coverage
- Growth of celebrity

Now repeat the activity with the following question:

'Media coverage was the prime factor in the development of an anti-establishment culture in Britain between 1990 and 1997.' Assess the validity of this statement.

Introducing and concluding an argument

Read the question below and look at the key points of the answer.

How good is the proposed introduction? How good is the proposed conclusion? How could either be improved to achieve a Level 5? Use the mark scheme on page 7 to help you.

How significant was the development of an anti-establishment culture in Britain between 1990 and 1997?

Key points

- Growth of satirical programmes such as *Spitting Image*
- Sleaze and scandal in government
- Laddish behaviour

- Environmental protests and direct action
- Scandals in the royal family
- Growth of celebrity and media coverage

Introduction

There is some evidence that an anti-establishment culture grew during the period of John Major's government between 1990 and 1997. This was due in part to the growth of media coverage that highlighted scandals both in government and the royal family to add to existing disillusion with the establishment. Media coverage undoubtedly showed its frailties – however, they had to be present in the first place. Major's government was beset with splits, for example over Europe, and scandals both in terms of corruption and sexual behaviour. Had these not been there they would not have given such ammunition to the media and satirists, who may have influenced public perceptions. However, there were other issues such as genuine concerns for the environment that drove an anti-establishment culture.

Conclusion

The media covered scandals and may have exaggerated activities in order to sell newspapers or gain viewers. It certainly added to the growth of an anti-establishment culture in Britain.

Foreign affairs: Europe, the Balkans and the end of the Cold War

Although John Major became involved in two conflicts, the 1991 First Gulf War and Bosnia (1995), the period was dominated by European Union issues.

First Gulf War 1991

Britain was involved in a short and successful war to liberate the Arab state of Kuwait after it was illegally annexed by Saddam Hussein's Iraq. Kuwait was liberated with the help of 45,000 British troops. However, Saddam remained in power and this would come to haunt Major's successor.

Interventions in the Balkans

During the 1990s, following the collapse of the Communist regime, Yugoslavia descended into civil war. In the ethnically mixed province of Bosnia, a policy of genocide against Muslim Bosnians was carried out by Christian Bosnian Serbs, supported by the largest state of the former Yugoslavia, Serbia. In 1995 Britain reluctantly became involved in air strikes against Serbian forces which nevertheless brought them to the negotiating table. Bosnia became an independent country – although the problems of the former Yugoslavia were far from over. However, Britain signed the Dayton Peace Agreement of December 1995 which, albeit briefly, stopped the conflict in the region.

Europe

The issues regarding Europe came to focus on the closer relations among the member states with implications for national sovereignty and potentially the creation of a United States of Europe. This issue split the Conservative Party during the Major years and beyond. The Maastricht Treaty began the process of closer political union.

The Maastricht Treaty 1992

Major supported this treaty – but many of his supporters opposed it particularly over the perceived loss of national sovereignty. The treaty envisaged – specifically – a common foreign and defence policy and the creation of a European Central Bank.

However, Eurosceptics became Euro rebels and openly fought against the Maastricht Treaty and closer European integration. In July 1993, they voted against the Government in its implementation. The proposals regarding Maastricht had been forced through Parliament in October 1993 – but the rebels called for a referendum on the issue, which the Government refused. Indeed Major was so incensed he himself in 1995 called for a leadership election. He won this comfortably, hoping it would reassert his authority. However, 89 had voted for his rival, the Eurosceptic John Redwood, and 22 had abstained. This showed serious doubts about Major as leader and indeed would serve to undermine rather than reassert his authority as he had hoped.

The 1990s became a time when directives from the EU were ridiculed. It was suggested, for example, that there were regulations concerning the curvature of bananas. Major did not support all the EU developments – he negotiated opt-out clauses, for example, from the Social Chapter, which was designed to protect workers' rights, ensure good working conditions and fair rates of pay. However, the Eurosceptics were less interested in detail than leaving the EU altogether. Major's government remained therefore seriously weakened.

Contribution and attitude to the end of the Cold War

Britain welcomed the end of the Cold War in 1989, although Thatcher was less keen on the subsequent reunification of Germany. Britain had remained a staunch ally of the USA throughout the Cold War.

(♦) RAG – Rate the timeline   (a)

Below are a sample exam-style question and a timeline. Read the question, study the timeline and, using three coloured pens, put a red, amber or green star next to the events to show:

- red – events and policies that have no relevance to the question
- amber – events and policies that have some significance to the question
- green – events and policies that are directly relevant to the question.

'The foreign policy of the Conservative government 1990 to 1997 was dominated by the Maastricht Treaty and its implications.' How far do you agree with this statement?

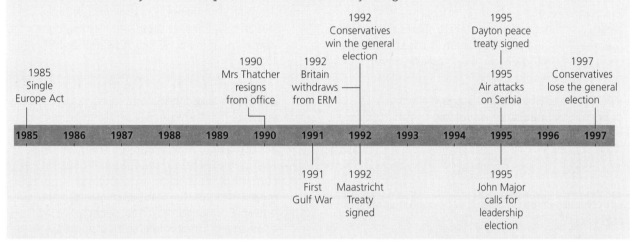

(♦) Eliminate irrelevance   (a)

Below are a sample exam-style question and a paragraph written in answer to the question. Read the paragraph and identify parts of the paragraph that are not directly relevant to the question. Draw a line through the information that is irrelevant and justify your deletions in the margin.

How accurate is it to say that Bosnia and Iraq dominated British foreign policy in the years 1990 to 1997?

It is in some respects accurate to argue that British foreign policy was dominated by issues such as Bosnia and Iraq, although the EU was significant too. Saddam Hussein annexed Kuwait, claiming it had always been a province of Iraq. This was clearly untrue. Saddam wanted control of Kuwait because it was oil rich, which threatened the interests of countries such as the USA and Britain which were huge oil importers. British involvement in Bosnia was more concerned with humanitarian interests as the Serbs were carrying out a policy of genocide against Bosnian Muslims. In both cases, Britain was part of an alliance involving the USA. However, although British involvement in these issues was significant, it was probably attitudes towards the EU that dominated Britain's foreign policy consistently over the period. Indeed the Conservative Party was split over membership despite government concessions such as opting out of the Social Chapter.

(i) Recommended reading

- A.W. Turner, *A Classless Society*, pages 17–46, 142–256 (2013)
- Mark Garnett, *From Anger to Apathy*, pages 266–305 (2008)
- Andrew Marr, *A History of Modern Britain*, pages 478–527 (2008)

Exam focus

On pages 87–89 is a sample Level 5 answer to an A-level question on source evaluation. Read the answer and the comments around it.

With reference to Sources A, B and C, and your understanding of the historical context, assess the value of these sources to a historian studying the implications within the UK of the Maastricht Treaty on European Union.

SOURCE A

From the text of the Maastricht Treaty of 1992; this treaty was designed to accelerate closer ties between members of the European Union. It caused considerable controversy in the UK, including among members of the ruling Conservative Party

RESOLVED to mark a new stage in the process of European integration undertaken with the establishment of the European Communities, ...

RESOLVED to achieve the strengthening and the convergence of their economies and to establish an economic and monetary union including, in accordance with the provisions of this Treaty, a single and stable currency, ...

DETERMINED to promote economic and social progress for their peoples, within the context of the accomplishment of the internal market and of reinforced cohesion and environmental protection, and to implement policies ensuring that advances in economic integration are accompanied by parallel progress in other fields, ...

RESOLVED to implement a common foreign and security policy including the eventual framing of a common defence policy, which might in time lead to a common defence, thereby reinforcing the European identity and its independence in order to promote peace, security and progress in Europe and in the world, ...

IN VIEW of further steps to be taken in order to advance European integration,

HAVE DECIDED to establish a European Union.

SOURCE B

From Nigel Lawson, *The View from Number 10* (1992); Lawson was Chancellor in Thatcher's government from 1983 to 1989 and an MP until 1992

In December 1991 at Maastricht, the European Union had concluded yet another in its seemingly endless series of treaties designed to promote the sacred cause of ever closer union. In fact with one exception, the integrationalist content of Maastricht was modest – more modest certainly than the Single Europe Act which Margaret [Thatcher] had, against my misgivings, signed up to six years previously. That exception was the agreement in effect to replace the EMS/ERM with full blown monetary union – a single European currency, later to be known as the Euro and thus a single European monetary policy ...

As I record in the main body of this book, I had always been wholly opposed to European monetary union, not merely as far as the UK was concerned but indeed for Europe as a whole. In particular I quote in Chapter 52 the major speech I made as Chancellor in January 1989 setting out the case against it (the first time this had been done by any Minister), and I continued to do so after I had left office – most fully at an EMU [European Monetary Union] conference in London in July 1995.

SOURCE C

From Ann Widdecombe, *Strictly Ann* (2013); Widdecombe became a senior figure in John Major's government, holding ministerial office from 1995 to 1997

In February 1992, Britain had signed the Maastricht Treaty which now had to be ratified by individual member states. The policy represented a significant shift in that it turned the EEC into the EC which later became the EU, thus formally recognising what had long been obvious – that the agreement was more than economic and it was not only Britain that was unhappy. France, often regarded along with Germany as being at the heart of the EEC returned a yes vote in the referendum with 51.05 per cent in favour. The Danes went further and their referendum simply failed to produce enough votes for ratification. After that there were some hasty exceptions drawn up and Denmark agreed.

The Brits went slow. We did not have a referendum but instead Britain was among those states which left ratification to Parliament and months of painful debate, uncertain votes and party infighting ensued.

These sources have considerable value to the historian investigating the implications within the UK of the Maastricht Treaty on European Union. Source A is taken from the text of the Treaty itself. It clearly states that the intention is to create a European economic and monetary union, with the intention also of a common foreign and security policy, with the aim in the final sentence of the extract to establish a European Union. The title of the new organisation clearly stated its purpose. In his memoir, however, Nigel Lawson feels that the Treaty was more modest than the Single Europe Treaty of 1985 and indeed only focused on terms of union in relation to the single currency. It is difficult to correlate this with the wider intention as exemplified in the actual Treaty. Lawson's view may however have been coloured by the fact that he had been Chancellor of the Exchequer at the time of the Single Europe Treaty and finance was his main interest. That he was opposed to closer European integration as such is shown in the phrase 'against my misgivings' when referring to Britain's acceptance of the Single Europe Act. In Source C, Widdecombe asserts that the agreement was wider than economic, implying the European Union implied just that – a sort of United States of Europe. Widdecombe was something of a Eurosceptic and drew the reaction of other countries into her implication – that neither France nor Denmark wanted it, as evidenced by the results of their referendums. In this sense she is asserting that not only Britain had its doubts about the concept of European Union – that Britain wasn't a lone voice among European partners in its opposition.

Introduction shows question parameters are understood.

Provenance of Source C considered.

The Treaty itself implied that it had been drawn up at the desire of all members. Its legal form suggested it was a response to the desires of the heads of member states. In Source C Widdecombe goes on to discuss its passage through Parliament. She mentions that the British rejected the idea of a referendum and therefore it required a torturous passage through Parliament. This was Britain's tactic to delay the progress of the ratification of the Treaty. However, the long process led to divisions and rancour. Widdecombe emphasises the nature of the delays, the opposition and its divisive nature. Her use of language is interesting with words such as 'painful' and 'uncertain' implying regret that a referendum was not held and the passage was so divisive. However, Widdecombe's reasoning outlines the problems with Eurosceptic tactics in that the delaying tactics led to divisions and party infighting. One feels she would have preferred a referendum, which would at least have been too quick to allow grievances to fester. However, she also indicates that the no vote in Denmark resulted not in rejection of the Treaty but some modifications that led to its eventual ratification. In Source B, however, Lawson as a leading politician from the Thatcher years mentions the Single Europe Act to which he was opposed and how he was always opposed to monetary union. This is a form of self-justification, especially when he quotes evidence in support of his stance, for example, his speech of January 1989. Interestingly he adds to the sense of self-justification by stating this was the first public indication of any misgivings by any Minister. Clearly while as Chancellor he would be expected to take the lead on financial implications he implies he had other misgivings too, which would undoubtedly have been repeated at the prospect of the Maastricht Treaty.

Consideration of tone and language.

Critical engagement with source but possibly some speculation.

Provenance in terms of purpose.

The Treaty itself is a legal document that states the terms of the agreement. It follows a pattern of internal logic, from the resolution to mark a new stage in European integration, to the decision therefore to establish a European Union. It elucidates the different aspects in doing so, from economic and monetary union to integration in economic and other fields such as environmental protection, and a common defence policy. It also sets fine goals such as the promotion of peace, security and progress not just in Europe but throughout the world. In a sense these are the words one would expect to find in treaties, setting out general aims and emphasising their value. The provisions of the Treaty need to be interpreted in terms of implications however – for example, it speaks of the need to implement a common foreign and security policy but goes on to see this as a step in the eventual creation of not only a common defence policy but of a common defence itself – which presumably means a European army made up of the military from member states. This would indeed imply a European integration far beyond the economic and would presumably be something Eurosceptics such as Lawson would object to. Similarly the common currency might imply formal economic and financial union at some point in the future – although at present it is seen as a stage in such development.

> Uses source to discuss implications.

> Uses source to see implications.

Both Lawson and Widdecombe are former politicians who may use their memoirs to justify their actions. Lawson in particular is anxious to impress that he always opposed monetary union and indeed references a speech to confirm this. Given that the Maastricht Treaty emanated from the Single Europe Treaty he is particular in affirming that he opposed this also. It may be that as a leading Conservative originally writing at the time of divisions within the party concerning Europe he is anxious to assert his credentials as a Eurosceptic. Widdecombe's writing is more dispassionate, omitting her own feelings but showing that it wasn't just Britain that opposed the Treaty. However, both politicians are writing from the perspective of hindsight and may have misremembered or be skewing the content in attempting to justify their positions. The fact that Widdecombe omits her own views might suggest she is trying to appeal to a wide variety of opinion in her memoir. However, one can infer that she regretted the lack of a referendum, as the alternative tactics of delay and obfuscation as the Treaty was ratified through the parliamentary process led to political divisions. Lawson however is commenting on a memoir he had already written in 1991, while his opposition to a common currency at the time of the Single Europe Act was very much a matter of public record. Both have the luxury of hindsight, with Lawson taking the opportunity to revise his original memoirs and Widdecombe writing in 2013, twenty years after the events. Widdecombe, for example, regrets the tactics that led to party divisions – but possibly the proponents of 'painful debate, uncertain votes and party infighting' did not know the extent to which this would damage the Government and indeed their party.

> Provenance in terms of perspective of hindsight, but could be developed.

> Provenance in terms of purpose.

Overall therefore the sources are all of use to the historian but in different ways. Source A is the text of the Treaty itself, setting out the aims in a legalistic form which suggests it is in response to demands from the heads of member states which by implication represent the views of their citizens. It asserts European union is of benefit not only to Europe but to the wider world, for example in its emphasis on justice, social cohesion and peace and security for the world. Sources B and C are memoirs from senior politicians: Lawson was a Eurosceptic who uses the perspective of time to justify his stance, reminding the reader of speeches he made to oppose monetary union. His perspective is rather narrow, focusing on the monetary union aspects which mainly concerned him as a former Chancellor. Widdecombe takes a wider picture, going into the political infighting that she was aware of as a member of John Major's government, fully aware of how damaging it was to party and government cohesion. Source B in particular illustrates how politicians can use memoirs to justify their stance, while Widdecombe appears more impartial.

> Balanced conclusion using sources summatively.

This response shows good understanding of all three sources in relation to content and provenance. There is a balanced argument in relation to the question. However, more could have been made of Source A, and the limitations of sources in terms of the perspective of time could have been further developed, particularly as B and C were both political memoirs that may have been self-serving. This response therefore remains within Level 4.

Moving from a Level 4 to Level 5

The A-level exam focus essay at the end of Section 2 (pages 39–41) provided a Level 5 essay. The essay here achieves a Level 4. Read both essays, and the comments provided. Make a list of the additional features required to push a Level 4 essay into Level 5.

6 The era of New Labour 1997–2007

The Labour governments 1997–2007

Tony Blair's government began in a mood of optimism, and enjoyed a halcyon period.

Blair as leader

Blair preferred to meet with ministers personally and eschewed long cabinet meetings. He appointed large numbers of political advisers. Critics argued he had adopted a presidential style of government.

Constitutional change

Devolution

Blair had committed his party to devolution for Scotland and Wales if their populations wanted it. Both held referendums on the issue in 1997, with 60 per cent of Scots in favour and a less than 1 per cent majority in Wales.

Accordingly 1999 saw the creation of Scottish and Welsh Assemblies: eventually both had the powers to raise their own taxes and run their own domestic affairs.

House of Lords reform

Blair was committed to reform of the House of Lords, which was wholly unelected and seemed an anachronism in the 21st century. However, the problem was how to reform it. The reform process began in 2000. Hereditary peers were no longer allowed to sit in the Lords, but they were replaced by more and more life peers appointed by the Blair administration. Despite various suggestions of 'a people's chamber' with peers somehow elected by popular choice, the situation remained. The House of Lords was at best partially reformed.

Northern Ireland and the Good Friday Agreement

The Blair government built on the work of its predecessor to bring peace finally to Northern Ireland. The Good Friday Agreement was signed on 10 April 1998.

Good Friday Agreement

The agreement made various guarantees.
- Northern Ireland could remain within the UK for as long as the majority of its citizens wanted.
- The Irish Republic withdrew all territorial claims to Northern Ireland.
- A Northern Ireland Assembly would be set up with power shared between the largest of the different political parties.
- All paramilitary prisoners would be released within two years.

The agreement was made possible by several factors.
- The British government was able to work closely with the Irish government under Bertie Aherne.
- Sinn Fein, the political wing of the IRA, accepted the need to decommission weapons, and the terrorists complied.
- The agreement was put to a referendum both in Northern Ireland and the Republic: in the latter, 95 per cent approved, with 71 per cent in Northern Ireland.

Problems

The situation remained tense for many years.
- A breakaway IRA group committed the worst atrocity of the Troubles in August 1998 when 28 people were killed in a bombing in the Northern Ireland town of Omagh.
- The largest Protestant party, the Democratic Unionist Party (DUP) under leader Ian Paisley, refused to join the Assembly.
- The Assembly was suspended in October 2002 because of the lack of trust between the main parties.

However, by 2006 the St Andrews Agreement set an agenda for restoring the Assembly with DUP participation. In the 2007 elections it won and Ian Paisley became First Minister, building up a strong working relationship with his deputy, Martin McGuinness of Sinn Fein.

The Good Friday Agreement was a significant achievement by the Labour government.

RAG – Rate the timeline
a

Below are a sample exam-style question and a timeline. Read the question, study the timeline and, using three coloured pens, put a red, amber or green star next to the events to show:

- red – events and policies that have no relevance to the question
- amber – events and policies that have some significance to the question
- green – events and policies that are directly related to the question.

'The Good Friday Agreement was the most important constitutional development during Tony Blair's term of office.' Assess the validity of this statement.

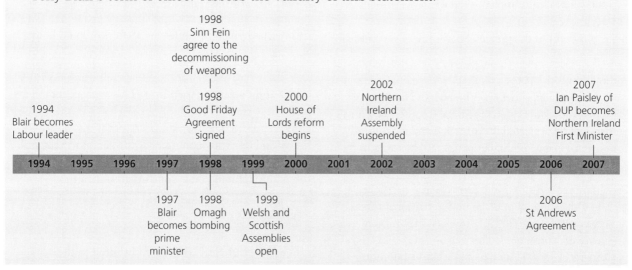

Spectrum of importance

Below are a sample exam-style question and a list of general points that could be used to answer the question. Use your own knowledge and the information on the opposite page to reach a judgement about the importance of these general points to the question posed. Write numbers on the spectrum below to indicate their relative importance. Having done this, write a brief justification of your placement, explaining why some of the factors are more important than others. The resulting diagram could form the basis of an essay plan.

To what extent was the Labour government of 1997 to 2007 dominated by political reform?

1 Constitutional developments

2 Devolution for Scotland and Wales

3 Good Friday Agreement

4 House of Lords reform

5 Economic issues (see page 92)

6 Foreign policies – Iraq (see page 100)

Least important ←————————————————————————————→ Most important

Domestic policies

Brown and economic policy

The Blair government seemed to manage the economy successfully. Led by Gordon Brown as Chancellor, it was a time of low inflation and unemployment. Brown appeared to set the tone immediately, demonstrating responsible management by:

- making the Bank of England responsible for setting interest rates, thus implying reduced government interference
- keeping within the previous government's spending plans.

Although income taxes remained low, various benefits were removed and other taxes increased. However, the Government accepted the Social Chapter which its predecessor had rejected (see page 84) and introduced a minimum wage and higher pensions. Spending in education and healthcare was maintained.

Brown moreover took some controversial decisions.

- When the value of gold fell on international markets between 1999 and 2002, Brown sold 13 million ounces of British gold. This was a mistake – as the value recovered, Britain had lost US $3 billion by 2005.
- To meet the shortfall in government spending he borrowed heavily from the banks – this meant problems in the later years of the decade when recession hit, as the banks demanded repayment.

Economic difficulties

There were various economic difficulties during the period of Blair's first administration.

Foot-and-mouth disease

The Blair administration was put on the back foot by an outbreak of foot-and-mouth disease in 1999. It had little idea how to deal with it effectively and decided on the wholesale slaughter of livestock and closing off much of the countryside. This led to considerable hardships for farmers and the tourist industry while many suggested there were far more effective ways of dealing with the crisis such as mass vaccination.

Fuel crisis 2000

In 2000, lorry drivers and farmers made an alliance in protest against what they considered excessive taxes on petrol. As they blockaded petrol refineries, the country came to a standstill. Within a few days there were serious shortages of food, people could not get to work and hospitals were threatened with closure. It may be that neither the protesters nor the Government had realised the impact their protest would have – but a settlement was reached whereby duties on petrol would no longer be automatically increased.

The Blair years were noticeable for high levels of credit and consumer spending. This was acceptable to a certain extent in times of prosperity, but in recession could, and did, lead to significant problems. However, the second term saw continued low unemployment and significant modernisation within business – although the manufacturing base continued to decline.

Energy

The Government had been committed to the development of renewable energy, with a target of its supplying 10 per cent of UK energy by 2010. However, this was over-ambitious, and controversially the Government began to invest in nuclear power to make up the shortfall.

Overall Blair and Brown inherited a buoyant economy for which they largely took credit. However, it was fuelled by credit and when recession hit in 2008 many people found themselves saddled with debts they couldn't repay, just as the Government found a deficit it could not meet without measures of considerable austerity.

Develop the detail

Below are a sample exam-style question and a paragraph written in answer to this question. The paragraph contains a limited amount of detail. Annotate the paragraph to add additional information to the answer.

How successful was the economic management of the Labour governments 1997 to 2007?

The Blair government seemed to manage the economy successfully. It was a time of low inflation and unemployment. Chancellor Gordon Brown appeared to set the tone immediately by demonstrating responsible management. Overall Blair and Brown inherited a buoyant economy. However, it was fuelled by credit. Brown allowed the bank of England to set interest rates. He borrowed heavily from the banks. Many people enjoyed a consumer boom. This too was fuelled by credit.

Introducing and concluding an argument

Look at the key points of the answer below. How good is the proposed introduction? How effective is the proposed conclusion. How could either be improved to achieve a Level 5? Use the mark scheme on page 7 to help you.

'The Labour governments handled the economy well between 1997 and 2007.' How far do you agree with this statement?

Key points

- Period of low inflation and low unemployment
- Giving Bank of England responsibility for setting interest rates
- Responsible financing – keeping government spending within agreed levels
- Sale of gold
- Heavy borrowing from banks
- Consumer boom fuelled by credit

Introduction

The Blair government seemed to handle the economy successfully between 1997 and 2007. Low levels of inflation and unemployment were maintained, and the Government was prepared to leave significant economic decisions to experts, as, for example, when Chancellor Gordon Brown delegated the setting of interest rates to the Bank of England. However, the consumer boom and indeed government spending were fuelled by credit. Just as the Government borrowed heavily from banks, so did consumers. There were also some controversial decisions such as the sale of gold in 2002. One needs therefore to look beyond the headlines to assess how effectively the Government did in fact handle the economy between 1997 and 2007.

Conclusion

In conclusion, the ten years between 1997 and 2007 saw low inflation and low unemployment. If you compare this with the 1970s when Britain was the 'sick man of Europe' the Government appeared to handle the economy very well indeed.

The Conservative Party 1997–2007: reasons for electoral failures

Elections of 2001 and 2005

Although Blair's three successive electoral victories were an impressive achievement, commentators noted some concerns.

- In 2001, less than 59 per cent of the electorate voted and in 2005, 61.4 per cent. Many put this down to voter apathy: Blair would win easily so there was no point in voting. However, others believed more people were disillusioned with politics and saw no choice between the main parties – they saw the comparatively low turn-out as a conscious statement that people had lost support for the political system.
- The Conservatives, despite having well-respected leaders, seemed tired and lacklustre and did not offer a viable alternative to Labour.

Conservative leaders and reasons for divisions

The fundamental problem with the Conservative Party was that it remained bitterly divided over Europe.

Leaders

- William Hague 1997–2001

In 1997, when John Major resigned, the obvious leader was the vastly experienced and well-respected Kenneth Clarke. However, he was regarded as being too pro-Europe to earn widespread support among rank and file members. Hence William Hague was chosen. Hague was associated with the right of the party, and during the 2001 election concentrated too much on his anti-European stance – the party therefore seemed too narrow to be considered a viable alternative to Blair.

- Iain Duncan Smith 2001–03

Hague's successor, Iain Duncan Smith, was rather uncharismatic and performed poorly in Parliament against Blair. He resigned as leader in 2003, to be replaced by Michael Howard, a former Home Secretary.

- Michael Howard 2003–05

While Howard commanded widespread respect and performed well in Parliament, the party lacked a real alternative agenda to Blair. He was replaced after the 2005 election defeat by David Cameron.

Reasons for electoral failures

There were several reasons why the Conservatives lost the 2001 and 2005 elections.

- If they criticised Labour's record of public spending, the Conservatives would be expected to do better; but the Conservatives were a party of tax cuts and reduced government involvement. This went against the consensus of the early 21st century when voters were already concerned about reductions in public spending, and schools and medical services seemed under constant pressure.
- If the Conservatives campaigned on their traditional strong areas such as law and order and immigration, Michael Howard had not enjoyed a particularly successful record when he had been in charge of them as Home Secretary.
- Put simply, the Conservatives were in a difficult position and lacked a viable stance with which to attack Blair's government effectively in a general election.
- The Conservatives had not recovered from the problems and divisions of the 1990s and never looked an alternative to Blair's government – if only because they broadly shared the same policies.

The fear was then that it was not that the victories resulted from the popularity of the Labour government so much as apathy, indifference or hostility to the system. The post-war consensus had been replaced by wide political divisions, particularly during the Thatcher years, to be replaced by a new consensus in the early years of the 21st century.

Judgements on the value of a source

Read Source A below along with the alternative answers that assess the value of the source.

Which answer will gain the highest level in the mark scheme on page 7? Explain why.

This source is very useful because it gives the voice of beleaguered Conservative leader Iain Duncan Smith who was facing disloyalty within Conservative ranks. It was taken from a press conference called specially to record his feelings as a result of disloyalty among fellow Conservatives. As such, Duncan Smith is seeking to vent his views to a wide audience, in order to place his concerns on record. It is then valuable as it shows his words as reported at the time in the popular press and one can sense his frustration especially at the end where the alternative to loyalty is starkly given. However, in giving Duncan Smith's point of view it omits to offer reasons for the disloyalty: indeed it may be seen as self-serving.

This source is very useful because it is reported directly so cannot be biased.

This source is valuable because it gives Duncan Smith's own words to show his reaction to the disloyalty he was facing in having his own MPS voting against him. You can almost hear the anguish in his voice. This is a very good source.

SOURCE A

Statement by Iain Duncan Smith, 5 November 2002; Duncan Smith was the leader of the Conservative Party from 2001 to 2003. This speech followed a rebellion in the House of Commons of MPs refusing to vote against a proposal to allow gay and unmarried people to adopt children. It was part of a personal statement given by Duncan Smith at a specially called press conference

A year ago the Conservative Party chose me overwhelmingly as its first democratically elected leader.

I have never underestimated the magnitude of the task before us, but nor have I flinched from my resolve that this is a road which the entire party must travel.

I have sought to do all this with courtesy, decency and honesty, respecting those who would like me to move faster and those who feel threatened by our moving at all.

Over the last few weeks a small group of my parliamentary colleagues have decided consciously to undermine my leadership.

For a few, last night's vote was not about adoption but an attempt to challenge my mandate to lead this party. We cannot go on in this fashion. We have to pull together or we will hang apart.

If we are to be taken seriously as an opposition, as an alternative government for this country, we have to work together.

I cannot allow the efforts of a dedicated team in Parliament or of hundreds of thousands of hardworking volunteers to be sabotaged by self-indulgence or indiscipline.

The Conservative Party wants to be led. It elected me to lead it in the direction I am now going. It will not look kindly on people who put personal ambitions before the interests of the party.

My message is simple and stark, unite or die.

Social issues and Britain as a multi-cultural society

In many ways Britain changed significantly during the Blair years.

Workers, women and youth

The population and the workforce

The population hit 60.5 million in 2006, having risen by 5 million since 1971. However, the average age rose from 34 to 39 between 1971 and 2006. The population was ageing and the number of pensioners doubled between 1956 and 2006. This clearly had significant implications in that more people were over retirement age so comparatively fewer people were in work to support them. This led to such an unjust burden on the working population that one TV drama-documentary envisaged a war between young and old.

Women

Women had complete equality in law and many had assumed in the 1980s and 1990s that they 'could have it all'. This meant families, children and satisfying careers. In 1997 for the first time there were more than 100 women MPs. The media referred to them rather patronisingly as 'Blair's babes'. However, there were still plentiful cases of the 'glass ceiling' and sexism in the workplace. This was particularly the case in areas new to equal treatment such as financial organisations and the police.

Many women found they were still expected to take responsibility for the larger share of housework and childcare despite having responsible jobs. To an extent the question of female employment was a red herring. Both women and their partners had to work to pay the bills.

Youth

Blair announced a 'New Deal' for youth, aimed at creating jobs for young people under the age of 25. In its first year youth unemployment had fallen by 40 per cent. By 2001, 200,000 had moved into employment as a result of the scheme. However, critics argued that each new job cost the taxpayer £20,000, a figure much disputed by Blair's government, and one in four jobs were temporary, many ending after only thirteen weeks.

How far Britain had become a multi-racial society

Immigration

One solution to an ageing population was to encourage immigrants. The enlargement of the EU in 2004 saw the entry of Eastern European countries such as Latvia and Poland with the right to come to Britain for work. By 2006 possibly as many as 1 million Poles had arrived, transforming many areas including centres of rural employment. Attitudes to the new arrivals were generally positive, although there were concerns about the pressure on local services, and indeed implications for the future as migrants became established and brought their families to settle.

Multi-culturalism

Britain was marred by a series of race riots in the first few years of this century, for example in Oldham, which suggested that integration had not worked. Some felt communities were too ethnically divided. Other harsher voices suggested the cultural values of different groups were too diverse for it ever to work. They cited in particular attitudes to women including the imposition of forced marriages and female genital mutilation. While clearly this was a valid concern and there was a growing concern with the radicalisation of young Muslims – the perpetrators of bombings in London in July 2005 were all British born – most criticisms were groundless. As a result, the Government passed the Religious Hatred Act in 2006.

Religious Hatred Act 2006

This Act was designed to protect people from being abused for their religious beliefs, although critics felt religious hatred was too vague a concept to be able to be defined in law.

Moving from assertion to argument

Below are a sample exam-style question and a series of assertions. Read the question and then add a justification to each of the assertions to turn it into an argument.

'Society in the years 1997 to 2007 moved towards greater equality of opportunity.' How far do you agree with this statement?

Although women had equal rights in law they still faced discrimination because

_____

_____

Despite legislation non-white people still often faced difficulties because

_____

_____

Multi-cultural integration appeared not to have worked effectively because

_____

_____

Equality of opportunity was enshrined in law but often failed in practice because

_____

_____

Developing an argument

Below are a sample exam-style question, a list of key points to be made in the essay and a paragraph from the essay. Read the question, the plan and the sample paragraph. Rewrite the paragraph to develop an argument. Your paragraph should answer the question directly, and set out the evidence that supports your argument. Crucially it should develop an argument by setting out a general answer to the question and reasons that support this.

How accurate is it to say that multi-culturalism was a major development in improving race relations and changing the composition of the British population during the years 1997 to 2007?

Key points
- Ageing population led to need for immigration
- Enlargement of EU saw large numbers of European immigrants
- Race riots, e.g. Oldham
- Legislation against racism, e.g. Religious Hatred Act 2006

Sample paragraph

Immigration was encouraged during the period 1997–2007 in part to address the problem of an ageing population. Up to 1 million people arrived from Eastern Europe. Generally they were welcomed because of their work ethic. When they brought their families to Britain however there was often pressure on existing schools and healthcare services. Multi-culturalism meanwhile was problematic as evidenced in race riots in Oldham and other urban centres in the early 2000s. Indeed the Government passed the Religious Hatred Act in 2006 to prevent people being attacked for their religious beliefs – particularly Muslims, who were often generally blamed for acts of terrorism such as the 2005 bombings in London.

Foreign affairs: attitudes towards Europe and the USA, and the 'war on terror'

Many believe it is on foreign affairs that the Blair administration will largely be judged.

Military interventions and the war on terror

Operation *Desert Fox*

In December 1998, Operation *Desert Fox* was the joint bombing of Iraqi targets to prevent Saddam Hussein's weapons building programme from progressing. It was hailed as a huge success.

Kosovo

Having withdrawn from Bosnia, the Serbs began a similar campaign of genocide against ethnic Albanians in the province of Kosovo who also demanded independence. Here Blair appeared the prime mover, convincing US President Bill Clinton that air strikes in Serbia were necessary to halt the Serbs' behaviour. However, the ensuing air strikes were not always accurate, civilians were killed and the Chinese Embassy in the Serbian capital Belgrade was hit. Although Clinton would not agree to Blair's request that **NATO** ground troops be sent to the region, the Serbs nevertheless came to the negotiating table and withdrew from Kosovo.

This may have set a precedent in convincing Blair that force could be legitimately used to prevent injustice – the **Blair Doctrine** was first elucidated in a speech in Chicago in 1999.

War on terror

Following the terrorist attacks on the US mainland in September 2001, the USA launched a war on terror – the problem was to find who the enemies were and where they lived. It was known that the Taliban regime in Afghanistan hosted Al Qaeda terrorists and British troops supported US forces in attacks there. There was a major hunt for Osama bin Laden, widely believed to be behind the 2001 bombings. However, while bin Laden apparently escaped, the Taliban were overthrown – although they continued to fight to regain Afghanistan and British troops were deployed there to help prevent this. Blair won applause from the US for his loyalty. However, it was to be sorely tested.

The special relationship with the USA

Blair undoubtedly renewed a special relationship with the USA over his loyalty in the war against terror. It is alleged that he insisted on British involvement in Iraq when US President George Bush was concerned that he might not get parliamentary approval. Blair has been accused of being Bush's 'poodle' but the **Blair Doctrine** that preceded the war on terror negates this view.

Attitudes to Europe

Blair was a keen supporter of Europe and was quick to embrace the Social Chapter, which laid down minimum standards such as the Minimum Wage. However, Chancellor of the Exchequer Gordon Brown would not agree to Britain joining the Eurozone, in which from January 2002 a common currency operated – he cited five economic tests based on inflation, trade and jobs it would need to pass and currently failed. Blair reluctantly acquiesced although he had earlier suggested a referendum on the matter.

Blair withdrew all the objections Major had raised about EU policies, and supported, for example, the idea of a European defence policy independent of NATO. However, he failed to get any rebate on Britain's contribution to the EU budget, which all his predecessors had condemned as too high.

The international position of Britain in 2007

By 2007, Britain was perceived as a firm ally of the USA in the war against terror, and a more enthusiastic member of the European Community than under previous administrations. Detractors however felt it was too close to the USA and lacking independent policies. Many less developed countries distrusted its intentions and those who saw the USA as an enemy felt similarly about Britain.

Judgements on the value of a source · a

Read Source A below along with the alternative answers that assess the value of the source.

Which answer will gain the highest level in the mark scheme on page 7? Explain why.

> This source is reliable because it was a speech that shows what Blair was thinking.

> This source is very useful because it is from a speech made in Chicago where Blair is speaking to an American audience and presumably wants them to get on side in the war against dictators like Saddam Hussein. Blair is making the case for intervention.

> This source is useful in that it shows what Blair is saying to his audience, and indeed more importantly the implicit message. The first paragraph makes the point about dictators and how they need to be defeated – but how intervention should act as a precedent for the future. He suggests that if NATO fails in Kosovo, this will encourage ruthless leaders in the future. It is interesting that Blair is making the speech in a US city where he is clearly campaigning for US support in intervention.

SOURCE A

Extract from the Blair Doctrine speech given in Chicago on 22 April 1999

Many of our problems have been caused by two dangerous and ruthless men – Saddam Hussein and Slobodan Milosevic (leader of Serbia). Both have been prepared to wage vicious campaigns against sections of their own community. As a result of these destructive policies both have brought calamity on their own peoples. Instead of enjoying its oil wealth Iraq has been reduced to poverty, with political life stultified through fear. Milosevic took over a substantial, ethnically diverse state, well placed to take advantage of new economic opportunities. His drive for ethnic concentration has left him with something much smaller, a ruined economy and soon a totally ruined military machine.

One of the reasons why it is now so important to win the conflict is to ensure that others do not make the same mistake in the future. That in itself will be a major step to ensuring that the next decade and the next century will not be as difficult as the past. If NATO fails in Kosovo, the next dictator to be threatened with military force may well not believe our resolve to carry the threat through.

Eliminate irrelevance · a

Below are a sample exam-style question and a paragraph written in answer to this question. Read the paragraph and identify parts of the paragraph that are not directly related to the question. Draw a line through the information that is irrelevant and justify your deletions in the margin.

How accurate is it to argue that foreign policy was dictated by the Blair Doctrine during the years 1997 to 2007?

> The Blair Doctrine was first elucidated in a speech in Chicago in 1999. It is interesting that it was made in an American city as many critics felt Blair was too slavish in his support for the USA in his foreign policy. Nevertheless Blair had very moral values and believed that injustice must be opposed. Indeed he had been more bellicose than US President Bill Clinton. The Blair Doctrine stated that dictators will back down in the face of force. He appeared to have learned this from the examples of Operation Desert Fox and Kosovo where air strikes on Serbia had brought the Government to the negotiating table.

Iraq

Background to the war in Iraq

Saddam Hussein, who was believed to be an enemy of the West and therefore a supporter of terrorism, was still in control in Iraq. His regime was targeted by the USA as a priority for regime change and Blair acquiesced. In September 2002, Blair announced to Parliament that Saddam had weapons of mass destruction (WMD) that could easily be deployed against western targets. The complexities of the situation are still hotly debated, and other European countries to whom Blair turned for support refused to give it. Many believed the question really was about gaining control of Iraq's oil supplies. Meanwhile an anti-war rally in Britain attracted an estimated 500,000 people. The Leader of the House of Commons and former Foreign Secretary, Robin Cook, resigned over Britain's involvement in the invasion.

Position of the United Nations (UN)

The problem was that the UN had not given sanction for any invasion of Iraq. It had insisted in Resolution 1440 that Saddam destroy any weapons of mass destruction in his possession but he had not complied with weapons inspections. The result as far as the UN was concerned was a stalemate. Many argued that non-compliance with the inspections did not prove the existence of weaponry; others like Blair and President Bush believed he must be hiding them.

Invasion of Iraq

US and UK forces invaded Iraq in March 2003. Saddam was quickly overthrown – but the result was a vicious civil war that has not been resolved since and unleashed new and brutal forces such as **Daesh**. Hundreds of thousands of Iraqi people were killed and international terror entered a new dimension. London itself was attacked by suicide bombers in July 2005 and many Muslims have been radicalised by the forces the invasion of Iraq has in large part unleashed.

Muslims in the UK

The vast majority of Muslims abhorred the violence of extremists, but many were nevertheless concerned by public perceptions of their faith. Many were also worried that it was mainly Muslim countries that were targeted by the war against terror. They were particularly concerned that young and impressionable people were being radicalised not in mosques or organised meetings, but over the internet.

Weapons of mass destruction (WMD)

One of the biggest problems for Blair's reputation was that no weapons of mass destruction were ever found. Many believe his evidence was fabricated. This was compounded by the mysterious death of a Ministry of Defence scientist, Dr David Kelly, who was accused of leaking information to the press about their non-existence. Blair and his advisers were accused of 'sexing-up' the evidence.

The Government ordered the Hutton Enquiry into Kelly's death. Its findings, published in January 2004, cleared the Government of any involvement in the scientist's death but was reticent on the actual validity of the war.

Many believe that Blair was seduced by the USA into participating in the war and contrast the situation with Wilson's success in keeping Britain out of Vietnam in the 1960s. Nevertheless, Blair genuinely believed Saddam was a threat to world peace and tyrants could be overthrown by force.

Analyse the answer

Read Source A and the paragraph provided that analyses it.

Highlight:

- the sections that refer to content and incorporate knowledge
- the sections that refer to provenance
- the sections that refer to tone and emphasis.

> Cook as Leader of the House of Commons resigned because he could not agree with going to war in Iraq. He is suggesting Iraq should be given more time to agree to weapons inspections and is giving his arguments weight by showing that other countries, for example France, Russia and Germany, want to offer more time. Prime Minister Blair, however, is more resolved to invade now. Cook's speech is dignified and measured, referring to international opinions and the need for multi-national agreements – and that the war on which Britain is embarking does not have these considerations. Cook is prepared to put this in stark terms: 'The reality is that Britain is being asked to embark on a war without agreement in any of the international bodies of which we are a leading partner.' The clarity with which this point is argued makes the source very useful in showing he could not continue as Leader of the House of Commons in such circumstances. Britain could be seen as an outsider in terms of the opinion of much of the world. Neither individual countries nor international organisations were in favour of war. Cook resigned with great dignity.

SOURCE A

Taken from resignation speech of Robin Cook, the Foreign Secretary in the House of Commons, 18 March 2003; Cook opposed a war against Iraq

I have chosen to address the House first on why I cannot support a war without international agreement or domestic support ...

French intransigence [stubbornness]?

France has been at the receiving end of bucket loads of commentary in recent days.

It is not France alone that wants more time for inspections. Germany wants more time for inspections; Russia wants more time for inspections; indeed, at no time have we signed up even the minimum necessary to carry a second resolution.

We delude ourselves if we think that the degree of international hostility is all the result of President Chirac.

The reality is that Britain is being asked to embark on a war without agreement in any of the international bodies of which we are a leading partner – not NATO, not the European Union and, now, not the Security Council.

To end up in such diplomatic weakness is a serious reverse.

Recommended reading

- Mark Garnett, *From Anger to Apathy*, pages 305–368 (2008)
- David Marquand, *Britain Since 1918: The Strange Career of British Democracy*, pages 376–395 (2009)
- Andrew Marr, *A History of Modern Britain*, pages 509–602 (2008)

Exam focus

Below is a sample Level 5 answer to an A-level essay question. Read the answer and the comments around it.

'Foreign policy during the administration of Tony Blair was the prime cause of social tensions among different ethnic groups during the period.' Assess the validity of this statement.

The foreign policies pursued during the Blair years between 1997 and 2007 were often contentious and led to considerable disagreements within society. However, to suggest they were the prime cause of social tension between differing ethnic groups may be overstating the case. Race riots in Oldham and other cities, for example, preceded the invasion of Iraq while hostile attitudes towards immigration and its impact was hardly new. Nevertheless the Blair administration may be largely judged by its foreign policy and its impact was widely significant both at home and abroad. It is therefore important to assess its impact on social tensions before examining other factors that may be relevant, and indeed to show how they may be interconnected.

States a case with evidence in support to anticipate the argument later in the essay.

Signposts essay in terms of structure.

In 1999 in Chicago, Blair made a speech that has been called his doctrine, or overarching policy. Having brought the Serbs to the negotiating table through bombing, Blair seemed to believe that force could legitimately be deployed to prevent injustice. In this case he believed the Serbs were practising genocide against ethnic Albanians in Kosovo who sought independence from Serbia. The impact of the bombing was itself a moot point, but, of short duration, it attracted little effective opposition within Britain itself. However, when the same principle came to be applied to the war on terror and invasion of Iraq, far more groups objected.

Possibly a little too much contextual background but does suggest its contentious nature.

There was widespread sympathy with the USA after the New York bombings of September 2001 although there was some disquiet at the speed with which Britain offered its support, and concern that its forces could become bogged down in Afghanistan. The focus however turned to Iraq where Saddam Hussein, who was believed to be an enemy of the West and therefore a supporter of terrorism, was still in control. In September 2002, Blair announced to Parliament that Saddam had weapons of mass destruction that could be deployed against western targets. Many believed more cynically that the question really was about gaining control of Iraq's oil supplies. Others, not just Muslims, felt Britain had no right to interfere in Middle Eastern affairs. An anti-war rally in Britain attracted an estimated 500,000 people.

Contextual background suggests division within society.

Nevertheless US and UK forces invaded Iraq in March 2003. Saddam was quickly overthrown – but the result was a vicious civil war. Hundreds of thousands of Iraqi people were killed and international terror entered a new dimension. London itself was attacked by suicide bombers in July 2005 and many Muslims have been radicalised by the forces the invasion of Iraq has in large part unleashed. In this sense the war in Iraq divided society not merely among those who opposed it on political or moral grounds but those who saw it more widely as war on Islam, or colonialism. That there was no end strategy after the overthrow of Saddam, and that British and US forces seemed to remain in Iraq as an army of occupation compounded the issue.

Maintains question focus.

Clearly there was a connection between the occupation of Iraq and the unleashing of terror within Britain itself as exemplified by the London bombings of July 2005. However, the bombers were all British citizens who had been radicalised at home. Serious questions began to be asked about the teachings of fundamentalist preachers such as Abu Hamza, and the impact of radical internet sites. These factors may have applied whether Britain had become embroiled in Middle Eastern conflicts or not, but there is little doubt they did offer a useful catalyst.

Shows inter-connectedness of events and factors.

However, other tensions emerged within society. One solution to an ageing population, for example, was to encourage immigration to enhance the workforce. This was particularly noticeable after the enlargement of the EU in 2004 which saw the entry of Eastern European countries such as Latvia and Poland with the right to come to Britain for work. By 2006 possibly as many as 1 million Poles may have arrived, transforming many areas including centres of rural employment. Attitudes to the new arrivals were generally positive, although there were concerns about the pressure on local services, and indeed the future, as migrants became established and brought their families to settle.

This pressure on services was exacerbated by concerns about the degree of success of multi-culturalism. Britain was marred by a series of race riots in the early 2000s, for example, in Oldham which suggested that integration had not worked. Some felt communities were too ethnically divided. Other harsher voices suggested the cultural values of different groups were too diverse for it ever to work. They cited in particular attitudes to women including the imposition of forced marriages and female genital mutilation. In particular it was increasingly felt that the radicalisation referred to above, and extremes in some views, was leading to a demonisation of Islam and adding to tensions through discrimination against its adherents.

As a result the Government passed the Religious Hatred Act in 2006. This Act was designed to protect people from being abused for their religious beliefs although critics felt religious hatred was too vague a concept to be able to be defined in law, and discrimination and tensions continued. It is of course difficult to legislate against one's beliefs.

While many believed Blair's foreign policy especially in the war against Iraq was misguided, it would be unfair to blame it for all the ethnic tensions Britain faced during the period 1997 to 2007. Society was changing and ideas had to change too to embrace these changes. While many non-white people felt conditions hadn't significantly improved over the years most supported the values of the society in which they lived and while the race riots of 2001 may have been shocking they were largely isolated and unrepeated. Nevertheless, the war in Iraq and subsequent occupation was divisive, and large-scale immigration as a result of EU enlargement brought challenges as well as positive results. Blair's foreign policy may have been responsible in part for social tensions but there were also contributing factors within Britain itself.

Strikes a balance in terms of question – considers other relevant factors.

Judgement well supported by evidence and argument.

This is a commendable Level 5 response. The structure remains tight throughout, and the conclusion is balanced, offering a well-substantiated judgement.

What makes a good answer?

You have now considered four high-level essays (pages 39–41, 56–57, 70–71 and 100–101). Use these essays to make a bullet-point list of the characteristics of a top level essay. Use this list when planning and writing your own practice exam essays.

Timeline

1950–51	Korean War
1951	Conservatives win election – Winston Churchill PM
1955	Retirement of Churchill – Anthony Eden becomes PM
1956	Suez Crisis – resignation of Eden
1957	Resignation of Treasury ministers over 'Stop–Go' policies
	Harold Macmillan becomes PM
	Treaty of Rome – formation of EEC
	Ghana wins its independence
1958	Race riots, for example, in Notting Hill
1959	Conservatives win election
1960	Macmillan's 'Winds of Change' speech
1961	Creation of NEDDY and NICKY for economic planning
1962	Commonwealth Immigration Act
	'Night of the Long Knives' cabinet reshuffle
1963	Britain's first application to join the EEC rejected
	Profumo Affair
	Death of Labour leader Hugh Gaitskell – replaced by Harold Wilson
1964	Labour victory in general election – Harold Wilson becomes PM
	Violence between mods and rockers at seaside resorts
1965	Rhodesia declares UDI
1965/1968	Race Relations Acts
1965	Circular 10/65 issued concerning comprehensive schools
1966	Wilson wins second term of office
1967	Second application to join EEC rejected
	Abortion Act
	Sexual Offences Act
1968	Theatres Act
	Dagenham sewing machinists strike
1969	Abolition of death penalty
	Divorce Reform Act
	Industrial relations White Paper 'In Place of Strife' issued
	Troops sent to restore order in Northern Ireland
1970	Conservatives win general election – Edward Heath PM
1971	Industrial Relations Act

1974	Imposition of three-day week
	Labour win two elections with very narrow margins
	Sunningdale agreement
1976	Resignation of Harold Wilson, replaced by James Callaghan as PM
	IMF loan
1978–79	Winter of discontent
1979	Conservatives win election – Margaret Thatcher PM
1982	Falklands War
1983	Second Conservative electoral victory
1985	Single Europe Act
1987	Third successive Conservative electoral victory
1990	Resignation of Mrs Thatcher
1991	Abandonment of poll tax
	First Gulf War
1992	Conservative electoral victory – John Major PM
	Maastricht Treaty
	Murder of James Bulger
1993	'Black Wednesday'; Britain forced to leave the ERM
1993	Murder of Stephen Lawrence
1994	Death of Labour leader John Smith – replaced by Tony Blair
1995	Murder of Philip Lawrence
	Dayton Accords concerning Bosnia
	Conservative leadership election won by John Major
1997	Labour win general election – Tony Blair PM
	McPherson enquiry set up concerning the investigation of the Stephen Lawrence murder
	Referenda concerning devolution
1999	Good Friday Agreement
	Blair Doctrine concerning intervention in foreign affairs
2001	Labour win second election
	Attacks in New York, 11 September (known as 9/11)
2003	Invasion of Iraq
2004	EU enlargement sees significant immigration from Eastern Europe
2005	David Cameron becomes Conservative leader
2005	Bombings in London
2006	Religious Hatred Act
2007	Resignation of Tony Blair

Glossary

Baby boom The period immediately after the Second World War that saw a temporary marked increase in the birth rate.

Baby boomers Term referring to the large numbers of children born in the immediate post-war period, known as the **baby boom**.

Blair Doctrine Tony Blair's belief that force could legitimately be used to prevent injustice, persecution or aggression within states such as Iraq.

British Leyland The final large-scale British car manufacturer, increasingly by the 1970s owned by the state.

Bureaucracy Those involved in administration and paperwork.

Butskellism Term used to describe the similarities in Conservative and Labour economic policies.

'Clean-up' campaigner Someone who tried to improve moral behaviour and attitudes, in particular by attacking the media which was perceived to be immoral.

Closed shop Where employers in a certain trade or employed by a particular firm had to be members of a specific trade union.

Cold War War without directly fighting each other as exemplified by the relations between the USA and USSR 1945–89.

Common Agricultural Policy (CAP) EEC agricultural policy designed to subsidise farmers who couldn't sell their produce by buying it at favourable prices. Britain argued this was wasteful and favoured inefficient farmers.

Conscripts Young men in the armed forces for a specific period of time.

Cool Britannia An attempt in the later 1990s to make Britain seem fashionable and chic through promotion of its popular culture.

Cooling-off period A period between the calling of a strike and it actually taking place when efforts would be made to negotiate a settlement to prevent it.

Daesh IS or Islamic State movement, who seek to restore the mediaeval state of the Caliphate in the Middle East with a fundamentalist Islamic government.

Direct rule Direct rule from Westminster introduced into Northern Ireland with the suspension of the Stormont parliament in 1972.

European Economic Community (EEC) European economic alliance introduced by the Treaty of Rome in 1957: it had the potential to develop much closer political co-operation and potential unity between members.

Eurosceptics Politicians opposed to or wary of EU membership.

Exchange Rate Mechanism (ERM) Precursor of an integrated European currency. The value of member currencies was tied to the one with the highest value – usually the German Deutschmark.

Falklands factor Term used to express the enduring popularity of the Thatcher government as a result of success in the Falklands War of 1982.

First past the post system Election system where the candidate with the most votes is elected irrespective of whether he or she has a majority of votes cast.

Flat rate tax Tax where everyone pays the same amount.

Flying pickets Groups of strikers who would arrive at centres of industrial disputes to prevent people going to work or movement of goods in or out.

Free market Economic activities such as buying and selling without government interference.

'From the cradle to the grave' Term referring to the comprehensive nature of the British welfare state, covering citizens throughout their lives.

Glass ceiling Discrimination in the workplace particularly in so far as a particular employee or group of employees (e.g. women) can progress, which is not formally acknowledged but usually well known about.

Gross domestic product (GDP) One way to measure the wealth of a country based on the value of how much it produces.

Hard-line Protestants Protestant groups within Northern Ireland who were opposed to any compromise with Catholics, for example, over power sharing.

Institutional racism Term referring to an organisation in which racism is so deeply embedded that employees cannot help but be racist in their attitudes.

International Monetary Fund (IMF) An international organisation designed to loan money to countries in financial difficulties.

Internment Imprisonment without trial, introduced in 1971 into Northern Ireland to arrest suspected terrorists.

Korean War War fought between Communist North Korea and its ally China against South Korea and a United Nations force to protect the latter.

Local shop stewards Local union officials who often had considerable power in their own workplaces during the 1950s to 1970s.

Marshall Aid US aid to help European countries recover economically after the Second World War.

Mass picketing Protests outside places where strikes are taking place, designed to prevent non-striking employees from getting into work.

Militant Tendency Radical left-wing group that infiltrated the Labour Party in the 1970s and 1980s.

Monetarism Theory that inflation can be defeated by increasing the value of money through reducing its supply.

National Coal Board (NCB) Organisation managing the coal mining industry.

National Union of Miners (NUM) Trade union representing miners which became more left wing after the election of Arthur Scargill as president in 1981.

NATO North Atlantic Treaty Organization The western military alliance dating from 1949.

New Britain Term to describe post-war Britain and changes, for example, in equal opportunities and the perceived decline of privilege and deference.

New Commonwealth Term to describe former colonies in Asia and Africa as opposed to the older white-run Commonwealth of Canada, South Africa, Australia and New Zealand.

New Labour Term associated with the reforms and modernisation of the Labour Party under Tony Blair, for example, abolition of Clause 4 (support for nationalisation) and embracing the free market economy.

New Right Ideas associated with less government involvement in the economy and people's lives with more responsibility given to individuals to manage their own well-being.

Pay pause Term given to a period of no pay increases.

Peace caravan A group that toured Europe in caravans to protest nuclear weapons.

'Permissive society' Term referring to the perceived liberalisation in the 1960s particularly in terms of greater sexual freedom.

Popular capitalism Theory that everyone in a society should have the opportunity to own property and shares in companies.

Post-war consensus Term given to broad agreement between the major political parties over policy in the three decades following the Second World War.

Private members' bills Bills introduced by backbench MPs.

Public sector housing State-run housing, often council houses.

Referendum National vote on an issue.

Royal Ulster Constabulary The police force in Northern Ireland, dominated by Protestants until recent years.

Satirists People who mock politicians and public figures.

Second-wave feminism Term referring to the feminist movement of the 1960s onwards who sought more than the political rights of earlier movements.

Sleaze Corruption and sex scandals particularly associated with the administration of John Major 1990–97.

Social Contract Term given to the agreement between the Labour government and trade unions over, for example, wage restraint in the late 1970s.

Sovereignty Relating to issues of where power lies: Eurosceptics feared too much power would be given to the EU.

Stagflation Term relating to inflation at a time of economic downturn.

Sterling International term for British currency.

Stop and Search Right of police to stop and search anyone suspected of involvement in a crime: it was used particularly against black people in the 1960s and 1970s.

Stop–Go Term referring to the use of interest rates to accelerate or reduce economic growth by the Conservative government between 1951 and 1964.

Suez Canal Canal cutting through Egypt to connect the Mediterranean with the Red Sea.

'Supply-side economics' Idea that the supply side of the economy should be encouraged, e.g. by taxes being low, and this will lead to economic growth.

Trades Union Congress (TUC)   The British organisation to which most trade unions belong.

UDI   Unilateral Declaration of Independence, the illegal declaration of independence by the white minority government in Rhodesia in 1965.

Unilateral nuclear disarmament   Where one country gets rids of nuclear weapons in the hope that others would follow.

Vietnam   Referring to the war between the Communist North and non-Communist South Vietnam in which the USA became fully involved.

Wets and dries   Terms used to describe those Conservatives who either supported or opposed Thatcher's policies: dries supported them.

White backlash   Term referring to reactions to immigration from the New Commonwealth by the Indigenous while population.

White heat   Term referring to the development of science and technology in the 1960s.

White Paper   Document outlining government policy and proposals on an issue.

Winter of discontent   Term referring to the industrial disputes of winter 1978–79.

Key figures

Tony Blair (born 1953) Blair was first a lawyer before becoming an MP in 1983. He succeeded to the Labour Party leadership in 1994 and with Gordon Brown introduced the idea of New Labour. He became prime minister in 1997, going on to win two further elections.

Gordon Brown (born 1951) Brown was a lecturer and journalist before entering Parliament in 1983. He worked with Tony Blair on the creation of New Labour. He served as Chancellor of the Exchequer from 1997 until Blair's retirement in 2007 when he succeeded him as prime minister. Unfortunately his administration coincided with the economic downturn, and he was defeated in the 2010 election.

James Callaghan (1912–2005) Callaghan worked as a civil servant before wartime service. He was a keen trade unionist. He is to date the only politician to have held the four key offices of state – Home and Foreign Secretary, Chancellor of the Exchequer and Prime Minister. As prime minister however he will always be associated with the 1978–79 winter of discontent.

Anthony Eden (1897–1970) Eden had been a widely respected Foreign Secretary who had resigned in 1938 over the Government's making agreements with Hitler. He was designated Churchill's successor but by the time Churchill finally resigned he was ill himself. His short-lived premiership was ended by the Suez Crisis, after which he lived as an elder statesman.

Michael Foot (1913–2010) Foot was on the left of the Labour Party, supporting CND and Britain's withdrawal from the EU. He became leader of the Labour Party in 1980 but struggled to assert his authority. He will always be associated with the left-wing manifesto that was partly responsible for the party's heavy defeat in the 1983 election. Foot was also a noted journalist and orator.

Edward Heath (1916–2005) Heath came from a lower middle class background, saw war service and entered politics in 1950. He was very pro-European. His administration was beset with economic problems, and after two electoral defeats in 1974, Mrs Thatcher replaced him as Conservative leader in 1975; he never forgave her.

Sir Geoffrey Howe (1926–2015) After military service, Howe became a lawyer before entering Parliament as a Conservative in 1970. He was Chancellor of the Exchequer (1979–83) and Foreign Secretary (1983–89). Noted for his loyalty to Thatcher he was later largely responsible for her downfall after he felt she had made his position impossible over Britain's role in the EU.

Roy Jenkins (1920–2003) Jenkins entered Parliament in 1948 and is chiefly remembered as a pioneering Home Secretary in the 1960s and one of the 'Gang of Four' who split with Labour in 1981 to form the Social Democrat Party.

President Johnson US president 1964–68 particularly associated with US involvement in the war in Vietnam.

Nigel Lawson (born 1932) Lawson was a financial journalist before entering Parliament as a Conservative in 1974. He became Chancellor of the Exchequer in 1983, and was associated with the economic successes of the later 1980s: some call it the 'Lawson Boom'. However, he resigned over disagreements over Britain's role in the Exchange Rate Mechanism (ERM).

Harold Macmillan (1894–1986) Macmillan was born into an aristocratic family. His service during the Great War gave him empathy with working people, and as a politician he always sought to improve living conditions. He was prime minister from 1957 to 1963 and remained a venerable, widely respected figure until his death.

John Major (born 1946) For a political leader Major had an unusual background – his father had been a circus performer and he himself was not university educated. Major worked in banking before entering parliament in 1979. He was promoted to key posts by Margaret Thatcher and succeeded her as prime minister. However, his administration (1990–97) was marred by scandal and splits over EU membership.

Margaret Thatcher (1925–2013) Thatcher was born to a lower middle class background in Grantham, went to Oxford and trained as a scientist. However, she fought considerable gender prejudice to be elected to Parliament as Conservative MP for Finchley in 1959. She rose through the ranks of the party to become its leader in 1975, and prime minister in 1979. Her term of office is still marked by controversy, but she is undoubtedly one of the most significant twentieth-century leaders.

Harold Wilson (1916–1995). Wilson came from a lower middle class background. He was a brilliant student at Oxford and became a senior wartime civil servant. He entered politics in 1945 and rose to lead the Labour Party in 1963. He was prime minister four times between 1964 and his retirement in 1976.

Answers

Section 1: The Affluent Society 1951–64

Page 9, Spot the mistake

This response lacks focus and there is no explanation of the post-war consensus. It risks becoming a generalised account of the work of the Conservative governments and even then lacks detail in support.

Page 11, Spot the mistake

This response doesn't directly address the question. Although some of the points are relevant, for example, members of the government looking old and fuddy-duddy, mainly the answer is a general account of why the Conservatives appeared successful during the period 1951–64.

Page 17, Identify the tone and emphasis of a source

This is a piece of journalism designed to be both informative and entertaining. It is written in the form of a narrative, with direct speech and a style intended to capture the excitement of the occasion – 'Suddenly … ', 'a fierce cry rent the air'. While this might achieve interest it limits its value as evidence because clearly the reporter couldn't reproduce the exact words used on such a tense occasion while some of the perceptions, such as children often treating the affair as a joke, would need more evidence in support. Here the desire to tell a good story well has got in the way of objective reporting.

Page 19, Judgements on the value of a source

The third answer will attract the most marks because it is balanced and comprehensive in its coverage, showing limitations with evidence in support. It also uses the information given about the source. The first answer is just about content while the second makes an unsupported assertion.

Section 2: The Sixties 1964–70

Page 25, Identify the tone and emphasis of a source

The tone is reassuring, with simple language an audience unversed in economic jargon could understand. Each sentence contains one or at most two points, to aid understanding. Wilson emphasises most people won't notice the impact of devaluation and it won't affect the value of the currency at home. However, he later contradicts this somewhat by saying that imported goods will be more expensive, but adds that this presents a good motive to buy domestic goods. From this one can infer the purpose is overwhelmingly to reassure the audience. However, the fact that this forms part of a national address suggests both the importance of devaluation and the concerns it engendered among the population.

Page 31, Eliminate irrelevance

The 1960s was a period seen by many historians as a period of youth rebellion. Most young people had jobs and plentiful sources of income. They spent much of this on goods specifically targeted at their market. Many older people saw their appearance and musical tastes as a sign of rebellion. This was exacerbated by challenging behaviour such as violence in seaside resorts and, later in the decade, football hooliganism. Seeing violence was threatening to the older generation especially when young people themselves couldn't explain it beyond the thrill it gave them. However, most young people weren't in gangs and didn't indulge in violence. ~~Even fewer became hippies espousing alternative lifestyles. It was however a period of celebrity among young people such as the model Twiggy and photographer David Bailey. These did become role models along with pop idols such as the Beatles and the Rolling Stones who enjoyed great success.~~ Most youth cults were a phase and most young people remained as conservative as their parents. Indeed most favoured traditional clubs and activities such as the Scouting movement, which saw its membership grow from 471,000 members in 1945 to 539,340 by 1970.

Page 33, Identify the tone and emphasis of a source

The tone is racing, passionate. Greer asserts her case rather than argues it. The language is rich, with phrases like 'deep desire', 'cage door'. However, the tone slows towards the end when the emphasis changes as she explains that women have achieved little despite their efforts. This source is clearly designed to persuade its readers that a new women's movement is necessary. In this sense it is useful in showing one influential voice, but we can't judge how influential it was. It is useful in showing the passion of a feminist argument but its reliability is limited by paucity of evidence in support of the points being made.

Section 3: The end of the post-war consensus 1970–79

Page 45, Identify the tone and emphasis of a source

The first three sentences are short and sharp, to make the point. Later the sentence beginning 'This gulf has …' is long in order to emphasise the longevity of the tensions, while words like 'exploited' are deployed to show how politicians have taken advantage of the situation. The tone is reasoned, explanatory. It seems that the author is asserting a case. However, he does suggest the barriers between working class Catholics are artificial and exploited by Protestant politicians for their own purposes.

Page 45, Identify the significance of provenance

This is a leaflet produced by the UDA, a Protestant paramilitary group. It is useful because it was produced as the Troubles worsened in Protestant areas which felt themselves under siege. Its purpose is a call for militarisation, suggesting there is an enemy out to destroy Northern Ireland and a need for armed defence. Its reliability in terms of factual content is limited because it is clearly biased in support of Protestant interests, but it does show the concerns that many people felt about the threats which both Northern Ireland and they personally faced.

Page 47, RAG – Rate the factors

Selsdon Man

The thinking of the New Right

The failure of the 1971 Industrial Relations Act

The miners' industrial action 1972–73

The growth in unofficial strikes called by local shop stewards

The imposition of a three-day week

The situation in Northern Ireland

The 1973 oil crisis

Economic problems such as growing inflation and unemployment

Page 47, Eliminate irrelevance

The Conservative government faced continued industrial action between 1970 and 1974. ~~It also faced problems such as inflation, unemployment and the 1973 oil crisis which ended the era of cheap fuel. Britain's economy had been dependent on cheap fuel. The oil crisis was a result of Arab suppliers cutting off supplies because they believed western countries were too friendly with Israel.~~ However, industrial unrest was difficult to contain as much was unofficial, called by local shop stewards by a show of hands often without even consulting

union leaders. The Government's response, the 1971 Industrial Relations Act, had failed because unions failed either to register or acknowledge the authority of the National Industrial Relations Court. In a sense this non-co-operation of unions was to dog the four years of Conservative government and from the outset was a contributory factor to its defeat in February 1974.

Page 51, Comparing two alternative answers

The first answer would attract more marks because it examines the sources critically to show their usefulness and limitations. It highlights the utility and problems with a diary while recognising that the Conservative manifesto is hardly going to be objective. However, the second answer tends to repeat what the sources say in order to consider its utility. It is a more descriptive answer.

Section 4: The impact of Thatcherism 1979–87

Page 63, Eliminate irrelevance

The differences in political policies grew after the ending of the post-war consensus which had seen a broad agreement on areas such as nationalisation and the importance of the welfare state. Mrs Thatcher was particularly scathing of Edward Heath who had conducted policy changes during his administration. She herself was an adherent of the ideas of the New Right, less government interference and expansion of the free market. Labour meanwhile had lurched to the left and advocated greater nationalisation, withdrawal from the EEC and unilateral nuclear disarmament. ~~Its leader Michael Foot was not seriously viewed as a potential prime minister while many still blamed the Labour Party for the failures of the 1970s, especially the winter of discontent, and feared a vote for labour would see the return of union power. The Labour Party moreover had split, with the SDP being created on a moderate platform such as continued support for the EEC.~~

Page 67, Judgements on the value of a source

The third answer would attract the highest mark because it is more detailed in its analysis of the value of the source, while recognising its weaknesses. The second response is a simple assertion while the first focuses on content without any evaluation.

Page 69, Judgements on the value of a source

The first answer is a simple assertion which tells us little about provenance. The second focuses on content. The third answer considers more about provenance noting its utility as a piece of contemporary journalism and recognises that the biased nature of Blackwood's comments could limit the source's utility as evidence – with example from the source in support.

Page 71, Analyse the answer

Source A is useful because it shows a private correspondence from Thatcher's ally President Reagan of the USA, where the president can be more informal and perhaps frank in his comments. **Here we see an observation about the intractability of the Argentinian leader General Galtieri combined with personal thanks for making the US envoy welcome. This hints at a close relationship between Thatcher and Reagan.** This is supported too by the first paragraph, which suggests the two leaders could have a personal discussion next morning. There is clearly a close relationship between the two. The letter does also however suggest Galtieri was in a difficult position, and feared any conflict with Britain would harm his relations with the USA. The letter is useful in showing that the US position was itself difficult in having two close allies on the brink of war. While Reagan recognised that Britain was one of his closest allies, he also acknowledged common ground and interests with Argentina. In this sense the source is very useful in showing how the USA fervently sought a negotiated settlement – which is presumably why Reagan sent his Secretary of State between Britain and Argentina in an attempt to broker peace.

Key:

Content and knowledge

Provenance

Tone and emphasis

Section 5: Towards a new consensus 1987–97

Page 75, Analyse the answer

This source is immediate, a reported speech in the House of Commons. Deputy Prime Minister Sir Geoffrey Howe resigned over Mrs Thatcher's attitude to Europe, **which he believed had undermined his own position particularly when negotiating over issues such as the Exchange Rate Mechanism. For Howe, one of Mrs Thatcher's most loyal supporters who had served throughout her term of office, initially during her first administration as Chancellor, to attack her leadership in such a way must have shocked many in the House.** It is also useful in terms of tone and emphasis. One can almost hear the sadness behind the

incredulity. He is saying it is impossible for him to do his job effectively with a leader who almost casually dismisses the case he is arguing with European partners. Also the cricketing allegory was well chosen in that it would be easily understood by anyone with any slight knowledge of the sport. Howe moreover goes on to widen the argument to explain how difficult it is for British businessmen when their potential clients have an image of a finger-wagging prime minister. The implication is that they become prejudiced against Britain because of Mrs Thatcher and the image she portrays.

Key:

Content and knowledge

Provenance

Tone and emphasis

Page 77, Judgements on the value of a source

The first answer will attract the highest level because it is objective in terms of provenance, striking a balance between partiality and what the author was trying to achieve. The second answer is generalised, there is no mention of this particular source, while the third simply describes what the author has done in order to discuss utility.

Page 81, Turning assertion into argument

The first answer contains assertion with some description. The second answer concerns an argument that while racism and violence were real their prevalence should not be exaggerated – and the Government did respond to concerns.

Page 83, RAG – Rate the factors

Downfall of Margaret Thatcher

Growth of satirical programmes such as *Spitting Image*

Sleaze and scandal in government

The popularity of the National Lottery

Laddish behaviour

Environmental protests and direct action

Personality of John Major

Scandals in the royal family

Growth of media coverage

Growth of celebrity

Page 85, RAG – Rate the timeline

1985	Single Europe Act
1990	Mrs Thatcher resigns from office
1991	Britain withdraws from ERM
1991	First Gulf War
1992	Conservatives win the general election
1992	Maastricht Treaty signed
1995	Air attacks on Serbia
1995	Dayton peace treaty signed
1995	John Major calls for leadership election
1997	Conservatives lose the general election

Page 85, Eliminate irrelevance

It is in some respects accurate to argue that British foreign policy was dominated by issues such as Bosnia and Iraq, although the EU was significant too. ~~Saddam Hussein annexed Kuwait, claiming it had always been a province of Iraq. This was clearly untrue. Saddam wanted control of Kuwait because it was oil rich, which threatened the interests of countries such as the USA and Britain which were huge oil importers.~~ British involvement in Bosnia was more concerned with humanitarian interests as the Serbs were carrying out a policy of genocide against Bosnian Muslims. In both cases, Britain was part of an alliance involving the USA. However, although British involvement in these issues was significant, it was probably attitudes towards the EU that dominated Britain's foreign policy consistently over the period. ~~Indeed the Conservative Party was split over membership despite government concessions such as opting out of the Social Chapter.~~

Section 6: The era of New Labour 1997–2007

Page 91, RAG – Rate the timeline

1994	Blair becomes Labour leader
1997	Blair becomes prime minister
1998	Good Friday Agreement signed

1998	Sinn Fein agrees to the decommissioning of weapons
1998	Omagh bombing
1999	Welsh and Scottish Assemblies open
2000	House of Lords reform begins
2002	Northern Ireland Assembly suspended
2006	St Andrews Agreement
2007	Ian Paisley of DUP becomes Northern Ireland First Minister

Page 99, Judgements on the value of a source

The third answer would gain the most marks because it goes beyond the superficial to examine the meaning. It also considers the significance of the venue. The second answer also starts to make this point but only as an assertion, without evidence from the source in support.

Page 99, Eliminate irrelevance

The Blair Doctrine was first elucidated in a speech in Chicago in 1999. ~~It is interesting that it was made in an American city as many critics felt Blair was too slavish in his support for the USA in his foreign policy. Nevertheless Blair had very moral values and believed that injustice must be opposed. Indeed he had been more bellicose than US President Bill Clinton.~~ The Blair Doctrine stated that dictators will back down in the face of force. He appeared to have learned this from the examples of Operation *Desert Fox* and Kosovo where air strikes on Serbia had brought the government to the negotiating table.